# PRAISE FOR THE TALENT BRAND

"Jody knows it all, from talent branding to culture videos to blogging to email marketing. Her advice is well worth a look if you're looking to embark upon any part of an employer branding initiative."
**Todd Raphael**, Editor in Chief, ERE Media

"Marketing and other executives who are not considering their employees as part of their engagement strategy are missing an important opportunity to create greater equity in their brand.
This book details why, but most importantly, how to leverage the insights of an organization's talent and realize an immediate and positive impact on culture and profitability."
**Heather Stern**, Chief Marketing and Talent Officer, Lippincott

"Over the course of the past 25 years there is one person who has been my 'go to' for any and all branding and talent acquisition strategy guidance – Jody Ordioni. She is insightful, fiercely bright, and one of the few who legitimately carry the title of Subject Matter Expert.
Few of her peers possess her breadth of experience and depth of knowledge. Her take on strategies, tactics, and approaches in this book will undoubtedly drive a greater level of success in the talent acquisition initiatives of her readers."
**David Lewis**, Chief Executive Officer, Operations Inc

"This is a timely and well-needed guide to building competitive differentiation in the talent space through branding organizational culture. Jody has done a wonderful job at presenting a well-written, easy-to-follow methodology that will help even the most novice teams deliver something truly useful for every phase of the employee lifecycle, from hiring through to organizational development."
**Bruce Stec**, Vice President of Human Resources, CQuence Health Group

Published by
**LID Publishing Inc.**
524 Broadway, 11th Floor, Suite 08-120
New York, NY 10012, US

The Record Hall, Studio 204,
16-16a Baldwins Gardens,
London EC1N 7RJ, UK

info@lidpublishing.com
www.lidpublishing.com

A member of:

**www.businesspublishersroundtable.com**

Printed in the United States
ISBN: 978-0-9987278-1-3

Cover and page design: Caroline Li

# THE TALENT BRAND

## THE COMPLETE GUIDE TO CREATING EMOTIONAL EMPLOYEE BUY-IN FOR YOUR ORGANIZATION

### JODY ORDIONI

LONDON MONTERREY
MADRID SHANGHAI
MEXICO CITY BOGOTA
NEW YORK BUENOS AIRES
BARCELONA SAN FRANCISCO

# CONTENTS

# ACKNOWLEDGEMENTS

*The Talent Brand* is a collection of learnings, thinking, strategy, creativity, and connections. Just as I hope it will enable readers everywhere to reach their goals, it would not have been possible without the help, efforts and support of many people who have inspired me to reach my own. They have believed in me and most of all encouraged me to think big, take risks, and trust that everything is possible when you start with "yes".

To the employers I've worked for, the clients I've worked with and the colleagues I've worked alongside, thank you for the experiences that have helped me grow. Specific shout-outs to Dawn, Fred, Geoff, John, Jason, Kathryn, Anya, Kim, Karl, Dana, and Ariela for their contributions.

A huge debt of thanks also goes to Cliff for connecting the dots, bringing me early opportunities and reminding me that curiosity is not just a sign of intelligence, but a key requisite for building great brands.

And finally, extreme love and gratefulness to Vincent and our family for indulging me, loving me, and allowing me the freedom to pursue my passions and live in Jody-land.

# INTRODUCTION

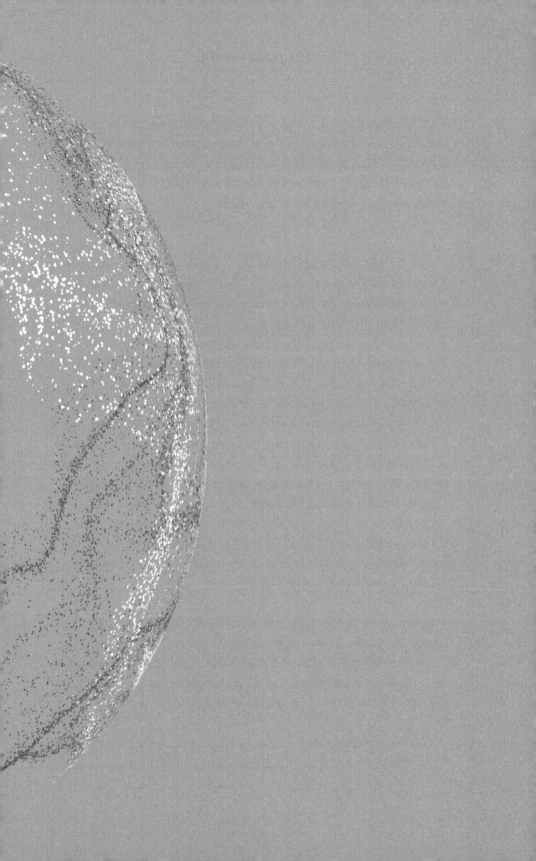

Time is moving quickly and organizations that are fast to change and seize opportunities are realizing greater financial rewards. And yet, the greatest barrier to change is creating understanding and emotional support in the hearts and minds of the talented employees responsible for achieving it.

## How can branding help?

The essence of branding is the successful alignment of the rational and emotive sides of our brains, creating rapid acceptance of new ways of thinking and acting.

Someone once described the optimal state of talent engagement as a CEO, a dog and a frisbee. Wherever the CEO throws the frisbee, the dog is there to catch it – running joyously, deftly changing course and returning it with a wagging tail. But now consider if instead of one dog, there were a thousand eager canines. Think of the impact we could have if we could harness such positive energy, and create such an agile army of talent, ready to pivot, change direction and chase down new opportunities.

If this sounds like the kind of impact you'd like to make within your workplace, then congratulations. You're ready to enter the exciting world of talent branding.

Your talent brand is the next iteration of your organization's employer brand. Aimed at branding the unique appeal of your firm's culture and employment opportunities, it also takes into consideration what people are already feeling, saying and sharing socially about your organization as a place to work.

If a brand is the promise we make to all audiences, the talent brand is the promise we make to employees and potential employees.

My name is Jody Ordioni and I am the founder and chief branding officer of Brandemix, a New York-based branding and communications agency. Our clients are professionals in a variety of roles, including human resources, marketing, communications, employer branding, talent acquisition and talent management, and they work globally, across a wide range of industries, including non-profit, technology, retail, financial services and healthcare.

They come to us seeking to create awareness, consideration and preference of their products, services or career opportunities and capture market share through branding. And despite this range of activities, we are able to deliver on these objectives because we employ the same best-practice branding principles and methodologies across all of the work that we do.

This book will guide you through our carefully constructed process, and provide you with complete access to the branding tools, templates and resources we use. It is my hope that it becomes a timeless and important resource for you and I look forward to beginning a meaningful dialogue and hearing more about your successes.

So, if you're ready, let's get started.

# PART 1

# BRANDING

# WHAT IS BRANDING?

Before we start with the specifics of talent branding, let's back up a bit and learn more about branding itself. Brands and branding can take many forms.

## Different types of brands

**Consumer brands** – Whether you're marketing direct to the consumer or reaching out to other businesses, chances are you fall into one of these categories:

- Product brand: think Apple, Nike or Dyson.
- Service brand: think AT&T, Visa or Bank of China.

There are subcategories too, such as luxury brands and NPOs (non-profit and not-for-profit organizations) looking to differentiate their cause and increase their share of donations, grants and volunteers.

**Personal brands** – Whether you're a speaker, a jobseeker or an entrepreneur, your personal brand will shine a spotlight on the qualities that make you the best choice for anything you'd like to do.

**Celebrity brands** – Celebrities shape what you think about products and/or services when you hear the name of the endorser. Athletes, actors and artists, and many other buzzworthy people, with or without talent, have elevated their personal brands and reaped huge rewards. In 2003, the soccer star David Beckham signed a lifetime endorsement deal with Adidas worth $160 million. In 2014, he made heads turn with his life-size figure that was placed on display for H&M. Which celebrities would you buy products from and why?

## Different types of branding

Just as there are different types of brands, there are different types of branding as well.

**B2C (business-to-consumer) branding** – Probably the branding that is most evident in our lives, this is the methodology that companies employ when trying to increase their client and customer base.

**B2B (business-to-business) branding** – This represents the efforts put forth by businesses to attract other businesses to their products and/or services.

**Corporate branding** – You don't have to be a Microsoft, FedEx or Google to implement a strong corporate brand identity. Along with marketing to consumers and/or other businesses, corporate branding includes the efforts of organizations looking to promote themselves to investors.

**Talent branding and employer branding** – At the intersection of marketing, recruitment and internal communications, your talent brand is a socialized iteration of your employer brand. It reflects your culture, reminds employees about what they love about working for your organization, and reveals to potential candidates what it is really like working for your organization.

## But what is branding?

The following is a good, general-purpose definition of branding: "The process involved in creating a unique name and image for a product in the consumer's mind, mainly through advertising campaigns with a consistent theme. Branding aims to establish a significant and differentiated presence in the market that attracts and retains loyal customers."[1]

In simpler terms, branding describes the method we use to decipher the millions of messages we receive each day, and how we categorize them in a hierarchy of importance. And we start this process at a very early age. A 2010 study found that while children ages 3-5 were not yet able to read, they often knew exactly which logo corresponded with which brand.[2]

Dubious? Then let's play a game. Look at the three symbols below and you tell me what organizations come to mind.

1   "Definition, branding," Accessed December 03 2017, http://www.businessdictionary.com/definition/branding.html

2   Anna R. McAlister, and T. Battina Cornwell, "Children's brand symbolism understanding: Links to theory of mind and executive functioning," *Psychology & Marketing* (2010): 203-228.

Did you say McDonald's, The Red Cross and/or Apple? If so, you've been brandwashed.

Here's what I mean. You saw a the letter 'M', a plus sign and a piece of fruit. Although none of these symbols are actual company logos, global brands invest billions of dollars in marketing to make sure they are the first thing you think of when you see familiar symbols. That's the power of branding.

**And branding is big business.**

Consider this: according to the 2016 Interbrand rankings,[3] setting aside the value of the actual company (assets, sales, etc.), the Coca-Cola™ brand name was worth more than $73 billion. That's the advantage they gain from their ability to create consumer preference and loyalty through their name and recognizable identity, and they also held the #3 position on Interbrand's 2016 Best Global Brands list.

On the other hand, Pepsi came in at #23 on the same list with a brand valuation of just over $20 billion. What's the $50 billion difference?

---

3   "Anatomy of Growth," Accessed June, 2017, http://interbrand.com/best-brands/best-global-brands/2016/

#3 #23

$73.1 billion

$20.2 billion

**Source:** Interbrand Best Global Brands 2016

Perhaps it's what we think of when we think Coca-Cola: Santa Claus, polar bears, Norman Rockwell. From early on, Coke has tied its brand to the imagery of America itself. On the other hand, Pepsi has been "the choice of a new generation", with previous campaigns featuring Brittany Spears, Ray Charles and Michael Jackson, to name a few. Are you old enough to remember Michael Jackson's hair catching fire while filming a Pepsi commercial?

It's also of note that from 1975 through 2010 Pepsi hosted 'The Pepsi Challenge', a blind taste test of the two sodas set up at shopping malls and other public venues. Pepsi emerged as the clear winner. So, all things considered, is branding the $50 billion difference?

Branded products sell at a premium thanks to consumer demand and loyalty. For further proof, look to the pharmaceutical industry, where on average the cost of a generic drug is 80-85% lower than the brand-name product.[4]

To summarize, the brands we wear, drive and even eat make a statement about who we are, and how we want to appear to the world. And as the competition for our time increases along with our choices of products, brands help to shorten the purchase decision-making process and leave us feeling smart, satisfied and secure.

And, of equal importance, brands deliver a promise to us. We form an emotional connection with the companies behind them, we trust the products and we come to expect the same experience from each of our interactions.

---

4   "Generic Drug Facts," Accessed June, 2017, http://www.fda.gov/
    Drugs/ResourcesForYou/Consumers/BuyingUsingMedicineSafely/
    UnderstandingGenericDrugs/ucm167991.htm/

# ONE BRAND – BRANDING vs TALENT BRANDING

Although this book is devoted to talent branding, in reality there is really no such thing. Your company only gets to have one brand. It's not as if you can have a consumer brand that targets consumers, a talent brand that targets employees and an investor brand that targets investors or donors.

The reason for this is that you only get one reputation.

We don't isolate our opinion of a company when considering it as an employer, a product maker or service provider. We distil, weigh and assess everything we know about a company and formulate one attitude toward it.

Walmart's dubious reputation as an employer doesn't just hurt its talent acquisition efforts; it deters some people from shopping there. Similarly, the Samsung Galaxy Note recall didn't just hurt the South Korean conglomerate's sales figures; it made attracting top software engineering talent very difficult.

There is a high correlation between consumers' admiration for a company's products and services, and their desire to work for that company. In fact, according to LinkedIn, North America's 2015 Top 100 InDemand Employers are Google, Apple and Facebook.[5]

It's no surprise, then, that these companies are among the top 25 brands in the world.

---

5    "Announcing North America's Top 100 Most InDemand Employers," Accessed June, 2017, https://business.linkedin.com/talent-solutions/ indemand-north-america-2015/

There is tremendous mutuality between a consumer (or product) brand, and the talent brand. In 1994, the *Harvard Business Review* wrote about the **service-profit chain**.[6] The underlying premise was that employee job satisfaction drives employee retention, customer satisfaction, loyalty and revenue growth. This relationship still holds true today.

Think about your own recent service experiences. Do you have a favourite store that you visit frequently, where the employees know your name and your buying preferences? What about the barista at Starbucks who knows just how you like your coffee? Doesn't this keep you coming back?

That's why the benchmark of a truly successful talent brand is how well it's aligned with the consumer/product brand.

---

6    James L. Heskett, Early W. Sasser, and Joe Wheeler, "The Ownership Quotient: Putting the Service Profit Chain to Work for Unbeatable Competitive Advantage," Harvard Business Review (2008): 413-417.

**How important is talent branding to an effective corporate marketing strategy?**

It's critically important. Here's why. Every company has a brand. Every brand has value. Millions of marketing dollars are spent each year on establishing brand awareness in the minds of consumers. But it is the employees who have the greatest power to make or break a brand. Employees shift the message from a concept to a positive or negative customer experience. Employees generate the energy and ideas that produce business outcomes.

Savvy Chief Marketing Officers (CMOs) are starting to pay attention to this. They're dedicating campaign budgets to setting up the Brand Promise – the consumer's expectation of the type of experience they will have. This is called the customer experience. Think American Express; think Emirates Airlines.

In some cases, it's woven into the message of their marketing campaign. "Shop here because our knowledgeable team of professionals will simplify the process of buying a car." Or vitamins. Or appliances for your new home. Some companies (like the online shoe retailer Zappos) may have a harder task of trying to create an exceptional virtual customer experience. But in each of these examples, success or failure lies in how well employees perform. And it begins with hiring the right people.

### What role can the head of HR play in furthering marketing goals?

If you are recruiting new employees, or even if you're not, talent branding plays an important part in the organization's broader branding efforts, and within high-performing companies there is a strong partnership between HR and marketing.

CMOs of large retail organizations often conduct employee research that reflects their desire to understand the customer through the lens of the employees.

They also understand that, thanks to employee discounts and their affinity for their company's products, it is the employees who might make up the largest customer segment within multi-store retail chains. As the face of the brand to customers, these employees are also key to bringing the brand to life. In these instances, HR truly comprehends how marketing efforts are furthering the business goals of the company.

But in other companies, HR may view the CMO or marketing team as a group that's typically too busy to assist with their talent acquisition or employee communications needs, and is only called upon to approve logos, colours and fonts.

To foster more collaboration between these two groups, start with knowing your organization's brand drivers and consider how they intersect with employee actions – either customer-facing employees or internal teams that support the business. (Think customer service, billing, etc.) Then make sure that employees know the customer promise, understand what is expected of them in delivering it and feel that they can personally make a difference. Remember that how we shape our internal communications can keep employees inspired to buy more or sell more.

## Where talent branding fits

As noted, talent branding makes a strong emotional connection between an organization and its culture, and the talent it needs to drive business forward. A powerful talent brand will help you reach the right audience with the right messages, to hire and keep the right talent to help your business achieve its goals.

And today, that's more important than ever. Unemployment has fallen to low levels. It's a seller's market if you're a nurse, an industrial engineer or a software developer looking for a job virtually anywhere in the world. And once great people have been hired, the work does not end there. It's just as important to retain them and to keep them motivated. According to the Conference Board, just over half of US workers said they felt dissatisfied with their jobs in 2014.[7] It's no wonder that when CEOs were asked about the biggest challenges facing their organization, they answered, "talent management".[8]

Hiring and retention have become increasingly difficult as we are bombarded with more competition for our time, and countless overlapping outlets and options for message delivery. Added to the challenge, we are marketing to a new generation in the workplace, and as we know, millennials consume, process and spread thesemessages in a completely different way.

That's why, as business leaders, we need to learn how to build a talent brand. This will be a critical driver in attracting top resources and fostering employee engagement.

---

7    Ben Cheng, Michelle Kan, Gad Levanon, and Rebecca L. Ray, *Job Satisfaction: 2014 Edition* (The Conference Board, 2014).

8    "The 3 Things CEOs Worry About the Most," Accessed June, 2017, https://hbr.org/2015/03/the-3-things-ceos-worry-about-the-most/

# PART 2

# THE TALENT
# BRAND
# JOURNEY

## So let's begin the talent branding journey

The talent branding process begins with carefully examining the organization, the culture, the internal population and the drivers of successful business outcomes. It also considers the latest and most effective media, methods and trends used to attract, acculturate and retain top talent.

The talent brand will become the backbone of your carefully crafted, credible and inspiring communications.

**To fully understand talent branding, let's begin by understanding the concept of employer branding.**

The term 'employer branding' was first introduced in the 1990s, and today has come to reflect the process of defining and promoting a company's reputation as an employer. Employer branding began as an effort to understand how current and former employees felt about their company and unravel why the sorts of people you'd want to employ would choose to work for you.

The factors that shape an employer brand include a variety of attributes: company culture, career opportunities and development, rewards and recognition, as well as the prestige of products and services and the very mission of the organization itself.

At the highest level of this employer brand construct sits the Employer Value Proposition (EVP), the single-minded expression of an organization's unique offerings as an employer, coupled with its expectations for employees.

And now that the world has become more social, and conversations that used to take place in the cafeteria are happening on a global stage, employer branding has evolved into a much larger practice called talent branding. The essence is still the same and the process still begins with the employees at its core.

**Talent branding considers what people share about your company as a place to work**

# TALENT BRANDING: WHAT IT IS

**Talent branding is the next iteration of your employer brand – the fulfilment of a promise of the employee experience.** It is informed by every interaction with employees in the organization, from pre-employment vetting to post-employment separations. More significantly, a talent brand is a dialogue of that experience, owned by every past, present or potential employee and visible everywhere.

Just as your consumer brand tells the public what your brand stands for, or a personal brand reveals what *you* stand for, a talent brand has the greatest impact on how your organization is perceived by its talent.

If the employer branding defines the promise you make to your employees, the talent branding reveals how successful you are as an organization at truly fulfilling that promise.

Here are a few things to remember before we move on:

## 1. Talent branding is more than a tagline, it's a philosophy

It's not a single sentence, or a series of vague qualities like *success* or *innovation*. It's not bullet points. It's not something as simple as an image or a colour palette. It's a framework built around the relationship between your organization and its employees. It's the promise you make to your workforce. It speaks to everyone, from the CEO to the newest hire, as well as to jobseekers who are approaching your company for the first time.

Much like a consumer brand, that sentiment can often be expressed in one sentence that serves as a point of entry for the larger promise within. At Southwest Airlines, it's: "Welcome on board the flight of your life." At IBM, it's an enticing question:

"What will you make at IBM?" At Pepsi, the talent brand is boiled down to one word: "Possibilities," which is repeated throughout their employee communications.

## 2. Talent branding is specific

Talent branding is not generic. It's much more than the overused, underwhelming phrase, "Our employees are our most important asset." A sentence like that doesn't set any organization apart; it has become a time-worn cliché that doesn't really convey anything. Even the term *asset* likens workers to computers or factories, which don't have kids or hobbies or career goals.

## 3. Talent branding is unique to your organization's culture

Your company can't just steal a cool talent brand from another company (or worse, a competitor) and apply it to it's own culture. The dissonance will confuse employees and scare away candidates. Your talent brand is specific to your company. It can't be applied anywhere else, since nobody else has your company's unique history, direction, values and goals. It reflects your special culture and represents all that your employees have contributed over the years. It's also specific to this moment in time. Additionally, talent brands can change as the company's mission, culture or goals change.

## 4. Talent branding is carefully considered

Talent branding is not cobbled together in a day. It's not something the CEO can write, send to recruiters and put into effect immediately. It can't be assumed, or conjectured, or copied from the 'About Us' section of an annual report. Talent brand marketing can't simply be 'good enough' or a placeholder, or something that can be put off until the budget allows. That strategy won't engage employees or attract the right candidates. Talent branding is created through a proven process. Often a third party with experience in the field is often retained to tackle the challenge with a field-tested plan and process.

## 5. Talent branding is difficult

Talent branding is not just a reinforcement of the status quo. Creating a talent brand isn't always easy. It generally can't be done by recruiters or HR staff, who have little experience in constructing a brand architecture and an employer value proposition. It's not something that can be handed down from the C-suite as a *fait accompli*, with no input from the staff. It's not simply art and copy that just 'feels right' or seems to match the company's eventual goals.

## 6. Talent branding is honest

Talent brand research asks questions about an organization's culture and the employee experience. Often, the process takes unexpected detours that can lead to brutally frank feedback and genuine discoveries. The result is truthful and accurate, and can help steer the right employees to your organization – and steer the organization in the right direction.

## 7. Talent branding is valuable

Talent branding is not extraneous. It's not a luxury for brands that already enjoy a good reputation with the public. It's not only for corporate giants or global brands. It's not an administrative exercise that can be dismissed as unnecessary by local businesses or non-profits. Talent branding is crucial to the bottom line.

Strong talent brands attract the candidates that fit an organization's culture. This reduces the chance of a recruiting mistake, which lowers time-to-hire. It also focuses the search on a certain type of candidate and increases word-of-mouth and referrals, which in turn lessens the need for large-scale campaigns and lowers recruitment marketing costs. A recent LinkedIn study[9] found that companies with strong talent brands incurred half the cost per hire of companies with poor or no talent brand, and one-quarter less turnover.

So, we see that talent branding isn't simple and it isn't superfluous. It's necessary, educational and valuable.

---

9  "LinkedIn Data Proves the Impact of a Strong Talent Brand." Accessed June, 2017, https://business.linkedin.com/talent-solutions/blog/2015/03/the-roi-of-talent-brand/

**To summarize, a strong talent brand will:**

- Connect people to your company's culture, mission, vision, values and career opportunities.
- Create a line-of-sight from your talent to their responsibilities and expectations for achieving your business goals.
- Demonstrate how working for your company is different from working anywhere else.
- Reveal the mix of rewards and opportunities employees will receive in return for their efforts.

**And a strong talent brand will bring you:**

- Better candidate quality and quantity.
- Increased referrals.
- Employer-of-choice recognition.
- Increased retention of the best talent.
- Higher levels of customer satisfaction and loyalty.
- Increased financial returns.

When talent branding is done well, your messages will become an inspiration and incentivise employees to become living ambassadors of your culture and brand, and passionate contributors to the success of your organization. They will stay longer, work harder, attract more talented professionals to join your organization and entice more customers to your business.

# THE TALENT
# BRAND
# ARCHITECTURE

Over 80% of leaders acknowledge that
employer branding has a significant impact
on their ability to hire talent.
– 2017 LinkedIn Global Trends Report[11]

Talent branding is not about starting from scratch or trying to conjure up catchy slogans that you think employees will find clever. Employees and jobseekers already have preconceptions about your talent brand because your talent brand already exists.

You already have a culture, a vision and values. Your employees already have a certain attitude toward your company. Your recruiters and hiring managers interact with prospects every day. You are already communicating to your employees and prospects through the images and messages conveyed through your careers site, social channels and job postings.

So, the talent branding process begins with curating these perceptions and communications and organizing them into the talent brand architecture framework.

11   "New Report Reveals the Trends That Will Define Recruiting in 2017," Accessed June, 2017, https://business.linkedin.com/talent-solutions/ blog/recruiting-strategy/2016/7-trends-that-will-define-recruiting-in-2017-infographic/

At the foundation of every talent brand lives the talent brand architecture, the structure of the talent brand from talent brand vision to the Employer Value Proposition (EVP).

The development of the talent brand architecture requires a careful examination of all the elements that comprise your business, brands, products and services, and how they each impact and interconnect with your talent strategy and culture.

So, it should come as no surprise that the framework can be visualized in the shape of a house since it provides the foundation for everything that comes after.

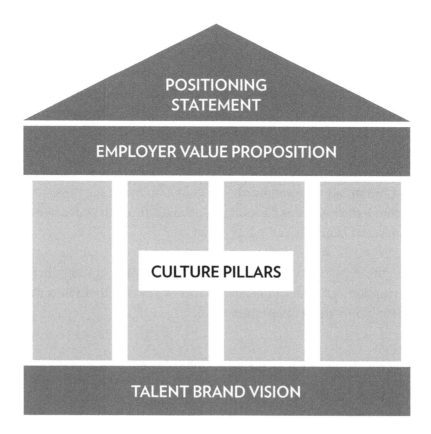

We build the talent brand architecture from the bottom up, starting with the talent brand vision. This aims to answer the question, "What are we all doing here?" The insight will most likely come from executive interviews and employee focus groups, emerging as a common-ground vision of the significance of the work being done.

On top of that foundation rest the pillars of differentiation, sometimes known as culture pillars. These are the two to four ingredients that go into your special sauce – the things that really make your company desirable as a unique and enticing place to work. These will be the themes that recur throughout your talent brand research and resonate with all audiences. These will be factors that make jobseekers perk up and that drive employee loyalty.

On top of the pillars rests the EVP. If a brand is a promise, the EVP is how you articulate that promise. It's a single-minded expression of the unique set of benefits and expectations that come with working for your organization. The EVP represents the most ideal – yet realistically attainable – culture for your company. It should be broad, passionate and aspirational, but grounded in the reality of your business and your values.

On top of the EVP is the positioning statement, visible in all employee communications, internally and externally. The completed talent brand architecture is perhaps the most important outcome of any talent branding project since it creates clarity, reinforces the value proposition for current and future employees, and informs every employee message and action moving forward.

# Employer Mission, Vision, Values and the EVP

There's a good chance that your company, even if it's a start-up, already has a mission statement, a vision and values. So, let's look at how and where these align with your talent brand, starting with the mission statement.

A mission statement should explain your organization's fundamental purpose in the world. It usually starts with "To be" or "To become", making it somewhat aspirational and evergreen. The mission statement drives business strategy and creates buy-in from everyone on where the company is heading.

Below are the mission statements (in full or in part) for the world's three most admired companies, according to *Fortune* Magazine.

**Apple:** "Apple designs Macs, the best personal computers in the world, along with OS X, iLife, iWork and professional software. Apple leads the digital music revolution with its iPods and iTunes online store."

**Google:** "To organize the world's information and make it universally accessible and useful."

**Amazon:** "We strive to offer our customers the lowest possible prices, the best available selection, and the utmost convenience."

The fundamental difference between a mission statement and a vision statement is that the latter is much more future-facing and describes who and what the organization *wants* to be.

**Apple's vision statement:** "We believe that we are on the face of the earth to make great products and that's not changing. We are constantly focusing on innovating. We believe in the simple not the complex. We believe that we need to own and control the primary technologies behind the products that we make, and participate only in markets where we can make a significant contribution. We believe in saying no to thousands of projects, so that we can really focus on the few that are truly important and meaningful to us. We believe in deep collaboration and cross-pollination of our groups, which allow us to innovate in a way that others cannot. And frankly, we don't settle for anything less than excellence in every group in the company, and we have the self-honesty to admit when we're wrong and the courage to change. And I [Apple founder Steve Jobs] think regardless of who is in what job those values are so embedded in this company that Apple will do extremely well."

**Google's vision statement:** "To provide access to the world's information in one click."

**Amazon's vision statement:** "To be Earth's most customer-centric company, where customers can find and discover anything they might want to buy online."

And finally, we must consider values. Company values act as a moral compass, describing how they and everyone working for them act in the world.

**So where does your talent brand fit?**
Sitting under the organization's mission, vision and values is the talent brand. As stated earlier, the talent brand describes what employees can expect to find and receive while working at your company. It also reflects the company's culture, its expectations of behaviour and performance, and its talent philosophy.

And while the talent brand is often used only as a vehicle to recruit new employees, it is in fact also internal-facing, bridging the gap between what people will expect and what employees will find.

Now that we've gone through the elements of the talent brand architecture, let's look more closely at the process of creating yours.

# THE
# STAKEHOLDER
# SESSION

The first step in building your talent brand architecture will be hosting a kick-off meeting. Bring together a team of cross-functional stakeholders, including colleagues from Marketing, Communications and Human Resources, to define your talent branding project goals and objectives.

Review and analyse any existing employee or benchmarking research and other relevant materials. Discuss the business case that is driving your organization's talent branding needs. This could be anything from trying to attract candidates, fostering recognition as a choice place to work, entering new markets, alignment with corporate branding or increased employee engagement. Though it may seem obvious, this is actually an important first step since it will help shape your research plan and discussion guides.

Working as a group, get answers to the following questions:

## Question 1.
### Who do you want to influence?
Determine who will be the future leaders of your business. While the talent brand architecture and EVP need to reflect the highest universal truth, we measure our success by how well it resonates with the people we need to influence most.

What are these people like? What personalities do they embody? Go-getters? Tech wizards? Idealists who want to change the world? Employees of your competitors?

This answer leads us to the second question.

## Question 2.

**What are the needs and desires of the people you want to influence?**

A recent survey of college seniors by Universum[12] found that they are looking for culture fit, work-life balance and opportunities to advance. So, if you're offering recent graduates lots of money up front, but little chance of career advancement, you'll need to change your marketing approach to make sure it resonates with the wants and needs of the best applicants.

There are plenty of workplace surveys out there, but you'll get the best information from talking to your employees, your candidates (even the ones who turned you down) and your applicants. Ask what drew them to your organization. What set you apart? What's still lacking? Accept the answers without judgment. You can't improve unless you acknowledge that you're not perfect.

**Spoiler alert: Answers to the next question may require collaboration with your senior leadership.**

## Question 3.

**What are you prepared to do to attract your ideal employees – and keep them?**

Creating the ideal employee experience could mean making some changes within your organizational structure or culture. You may have to increase perks, change policies or even enhance your workplace with, say, a gym or daycare centre or coffee bar. And that can't happen without the approval of your senior leadership,

---

12  "What do Graduates Look for in an Employer?" Accessed April, 2017, http://universumglobal.com/articles/2017/05/graduates-look-employer/

who may not see the need for such workplace enhancements (and costs). You can tell them that more engaged employees will lead to higher retention, lower hiring costs, higher productivity, and eventually greater profits – all true.

**Every company wants to have a talent brand that positions them as an employer of choice. Who wouldn't want to have talent competing to join their team instead of the other way around? Here is a list of some attributes that are common among preferred employers. How does your company stack up?**

1. Interesting work – Challenging but not brutally difficult; straightforward but not necessarily easy. Most workers want to be stimulated, excited or inspired by their work. No matter what your industry, are your positions actually interesting? Do they ask too much or too little of employees?

2. Career advancement – If you want workers to stay with you for their entire careers, you have to *give* them a career. This includes a clear path to promotions, regular and fair evaluations, and training for new skills. And don't forget about mentoring programmes, which are often lacking at many companies.

3. Social responsibility – Many people want to feel that they're doing good. If your company isn't part of the rainforest-saving movement, you can still recycle, partner with a charity and engage in fundraising activities. This attribute also includes business ethics.

4. Recognition – Not just about fair pay but also encompasses rewards for work well done and for time spent with the company. Contests (such as sales challenges) also help employees feel valued, as can bonuses, free food and other perks.

## Question 4.
### What is your talent philosophy?
Defining your talent philosophy will paint a complete picture of the types of people you need to drive the business forward and how they will be identified, developed, recognized and rewarded for their performance.

## Question 5.
### What does success look like?
Identify the project's success metrics. How will you know you've succeeded? Discuss and agree upon the measurements you'll use to evaluate your success.

Now fill out the **Talent Branding Brief**.

## Talent Branding Brief

Primary goals of the talent branding initiative.

Timeline for the project.

Budget for the project.

Do you currently have a talent brand? If so, provide information on when it was implemented and why you are looking to change it.

Do you currently have consumer brand positioning/identity guidelines? If so, please include herein.

Who are your target audiences for the talent branding initiative?

What are the most difficult-to-fill positions, and where are they located?

Who do you compete with for talent?

What are the primary reasons people choose to join your organization?

What are the primary reasons employees leave?

How many people did you hire last year?

What is your current turnover rate?

What are the rewards of a career in the organization (personal growth, advancement opportunity, compensation, tuition reimbursement)?

What recruiting obstacles are you facing?

Add any additional information that would be relevant and helpful as you work through your talent branding research project.

# THREE THINGS TO KNOW BEFORE YOU START

## 1. Start with the end in mind

**Identify key areas of the business you want to improve based on your Talent Brand, such as:**

- Recruitment.
- Selection.
- Retention.
- Employee Engagement.

Effective employee engagement leads to employees who stay, perform and recommend the company to other applicants. More importantly, according to Gallup, companies with higher employee engagement can outperform their peers by 147% in earnings per share.[10]

**Based on the areas you choose to target for improvement, agree on appropriate metrics to evaluate your success.** Set goals in advance and work toward measuring and refining them as you go along. Initial numbers or scores are not as important as making sure you're improving over time.

Rather than using *HR* metrics – such as how long it takes to fill job openings (time-to-fill) or what the average cost is to hire an employee (cost-per-hire) – consider tracking *business* metrics such as customer acquisition and engagement, same-store sales growth, shareholder value or customer satisfaction.

---

10 "The Engaged Workplace." Accessed June, 2017, http://www.gallup.com/services/190118/engaged-workplace.aspx/

## 2. Don't treat this as an HR project

Talent branding is part of your corporate brand and needs the involvement of your communications and branding teams.

It also takes the strength and support of a leadership team to drive adoption, build momentum and get it off the ground.

It's equally important to refine the strategies and messages to meet the needs of a global enterprise. Make sure that your brand architecture is consistent across the board, and that your messages are tailored to each audience but done in such a way that you're still speaking with one voice.

## 3. This is not a one-and-done event!

Talent branding is a philosophy and a framework built around the relationship between your organization and its employees (and potential ones too). If you don't weave this into the fabric of your operation and follow through on the talent brand experience, it will have an equally potent negative effect that can overshadow all your efforts.

# CONDUCTING YOUR TALENT BRAND RESEARCH

Your talent brand deserves the same study and due diligence as any other major decision your company makes. You need to go beyond theory and acquire actionable, game-changing insights that drive sustainable business results. That requires brand research.

Talent brand research asks questions that provide insight into an organization's culture and the employee experience. Sometimes the responses may reveal internal feuds, poor communication or general discontent, but the goal is to simply get to the truth. How do people really feel about working for your company?

Talent brand research helps you to discover:

- The real reasons people work at your company and stay there.
- What actually differentiates you from your competition, as a company and an employer.
- How to define and validate the current culture.
- How employees deliver the company brand.
- What may have to change for your company to really embody its talent brand through the organization's culture, attitude and actions.

There are many options to choose from and a number of factors to consider when crafting the perfect research plan for your talent branding initiative. But one important piece of advice is to use an independent party to do the research for you. As an employee of the company, there are just too many personal points of view you will bring to the research. Along with that, the key ingredient for yielding the best intelligence comes from people feeling free to express their honest opinions, rather than toe the party line. If you are a manager or colleague of the people you've selected to participate, there's a greater chance that they will tell you what they think you want to hear.

## Types of research

**Interviews:** One-on-one interviews are an excellent way to gather insights from individual constituents who may carry significant weight or influence on your project. These audiences could include customers, vendors, recruiters' candidates who turned down your offers, or former employees who you'd like to win back. But the interviews we consider most important are executive interviews.

**Focus groups:** You'll also want to engage small groups of people via focus groups. This can be done in person or online and can happen in advance of your surveys to help shape the ultimate survey questions. Focus groups are also an excellent way of testing the brand architecture after it's been developed.

**Surveys:** Because you want the process to be as inclusive as possible, you'll want to include surveys sampling your current employees along with those who you may be looking to bring on board over the next 12 months.

**Competitive audit:** The final element in most research plans is an external audit of the competition for talent. This can be easily accomplished by going to company careers sites, company-managed social media sites, and social sites that feature unfiltered employer/workplace conversations, such as Glassdoor, LinkedIn and Indeed.

Let's take an in-depth look at each of these research types.

Uncovering brand culture

# EXECUTIVE INTERVIEWS

A successful talent brand must connect employees to their role in achieving the strategic initiatives of the business, and its widest adoption will come from high-level sponsorship of these efforts. So, what better place to begin your research than through executive interviews?

The goal of the executive interview is to understand the business goals that drive the talent needs and uncover where the organization is heading, as well as the potential impact on the culture (present and future) and hiring.

## Who to invite:

When arranging executive interviews, the more people you can get to participate, the better the results will be. The following titles, while not exhaustive, are a good starting point: CEO/President, Chief Operating Officer, Chief Financial Officer, Chief Marketing Officer/VP Marketing, Chief Human Resources/VPHR, S/VP Internal Communications, S/VP Talent Acquisition, S/VP Sales. Of course, each project has its own nuances. For instance, if you're looking for greater engagement or more résumés from technology professionals, you'd certainly want to include your Chief Technology Officer (CTO).

Typically, these interviews will last 30-40 minutes, and can be conducted either in person or over the phone. As a rule of thumb, don't reveal the questions in advance because you don't want to give your subjects time to overthink their answers. The spontaneity of their responses will bring honesty and authenticity to your research. And since these are the people charged with driving the business forward, executive interviews will also bring a tremendous amount of passionate and inspirational content for you to curate and embed in all future materials. See the Appendix for a sample Executive Interview Discussion Guide.

# EMPLOYEE
# FOCUS GROUPS

The goal of employee focus groups is to build consensus, capture employee testimonials or stories and collect and validate information that impacts the talent brand architecture.

A typical focus group might involve between 8 and 12 people and last anywhere from 1½ to 2 hours. It's inadvisable to include more participants because, on the one hand, you're trying to encourage conversation and sharing of opinions, yet on the other hand, with more than 12 people it will take longer to listen to everyone's response and you may not be able to hold everyone's attention.

## Who to invite:

This will vary based your goals and the unique needs of your organization. Think about where the high-performing teams are and align this with your talent needs. Who do you need in order to successfully meet your business goals? Are there pockets of disengaged employees? Make sure you include them too, because this will help secure their commitment to the final outputs. And finally, include your sales and customer service teams. Your sales teams will be particularly important, because they are on the front lines, interacting with potential customers and representing the unique value your services and goods represent in the marketplace. Lining up the consumer value proposition with the EVP is much easier when you have input from the sales teams. The customer service teams will also be key participants because they hear first-hand what your customers want, need and complain about. These insights will add clarity to what needs to change as a result of the talent brand you are creating.

Employees can be offered a small incentive to participate, something that typically has a value of $25. If cost is a barrier, a free lunch can work just as well.

It is best to work with an external facilitator to ensure the authenticity of your respondents and protect their privacy. Ensure that the discussions are recorded (audio or video) or at least documented by an efficient scribe.

The flow of the focus group should start with a brief introduction explaining who you are and the purpose of the exercise. Make sure you include the instructions and housekeeping points: everyone should participate, there should be no side conversations and, most importantly, nothing discussed should leave the room.

The next step should be some kind of icebreaker exercise that ties back into the project. For example, you could set a pre-meeting 'homework' assignment. Ask the participants to look through magazines, cut out and bring in words, phrases or images that evoke how they feel at work. Then ask them to tape these snippets to the wall and give a brief explanation of why they've chosen their selections.

And finally, get to the heart of the session. Ask participants what is important to them when evaluating a company for employment opportunities. Do they feel that their work experience is meeting their expectations and why/why not? How would they describe the organization to someone who was unfamiliar with it? Where would they work if the company didn't exist, and why? What does a great day look like? Where do they see themselves going within the organization? Will they still be there in three years? Are they happier now than when they first joined? Would they recommend the company to a friend?

Refer to the Appendix for a sample Focus Group Discussion Guide, along with some additional icebreakers.

One final thought on focus groups: they can be conducted online instead of in person, and can be incorporated into any and every part of your research – before, during or after you develop the talent brand architecture and creative concepts. You can invite different groups of people to participate, or stay with the same people through each phase and measure if and how their sentiments may have changed throughout their involvement. Be sure to recognize and reward these people for their efforts. In many cases, this pool of people will become your future brand ambassadors.

# TALENT BRAND SURVEYS

Talent brand surveys should be a staple of any branding project. Yet when I propose this as part of a project plan I am frequently met with the argument that employees are over-surveyed, or that the organization has recently conducted employee engagement or other similar surveys.

Don't be dissuaded. Talent brand surveys should be a centrepiece of any branding project. Here's why:

**They are incredibly revealing.** The more people involved in a talent branding project the better. Information can be dissected, sliced, diced, validated and segmented by function, tenure, geography or pretty much any way you can imagine. This means that when the time comes to create content, you can personalize it to your audience and be as authentic as possible.

**They are consensus builders.** People really appreciate being involved, offering their input and having a stake in the initiative. Best of all, they are less likely to object to an outcome they had a hand in creating.

**They keep the project on true north.** While focus groups and interviews provide valuable insight, surveys validate them. Your talent brand architecture must ring true at the highest levels and the surveys are the best way of making that happen. While you can segment messages with parts and pieces that are true for certain populations, the EVP will be what resonates at the top of the pyramid. It's something that was informed and validated by the very people you want to engage.

**They really are different.** Typically, employee engagement surveys reveal sentiments about an individual's job, manager or prospects for advancement. Talent brand surveys reveal sentiments and emotions – what people feel is inspiring about the company, its culture, its mission and often its advertising and media work.

The best time to introduce the survey into the process is after you've held an ideation event, such as the kick-off we mentioned earlier, and finished your executive interviews and focus groups.

This allows you to address any lingering questions or concerns before you begin to assemble the talent brand architecture. You may find that instead of the three or four things that you thought were unique about the company's culture, you've come up with more attributes than you'd imagined. Conducting a survey at this stage allows you to test the pillars among your audience, find out which ones might resonate most compellingly with everyone and move forward with those. And don't forget to save all the information for when you get to the segmentation stage.

Refer to the Appendix for some additional sample Employee Survey Questions.

# EXTERNAL
# RESEARCH

It should be noted that research doesn't need to be exclusive to employees. It is an excellent way of finding out what people outside your organization think about your talent brand. It can also offer comparative insights about your company versus your competition.

Are you looking for more recent graduates, software engineers or clinicians? What do they know about you and how accurate are their perceptions? Which organizations do they hold in high esteem, and why? What are they looking for in their career and how close are you to delivering what they want? Which thought-leaders are they following? How do they feel about your current recruitment messages or social sites?

The easiest and most inexpensive external research approach is to reach out to people who recently turned down employment offers. Ask them for 30 minutes of their time and let them know that their efforts will help in the development of a strong talent brand for the organization. Also assure them that anything they say will be held in the strictest confidence.

Keep the questions general at first:

- What they are looking for in a career?
- What brought them to their current role?
- Who would they wish to work for if their current company closed its doors, and why?

Then you can go into a more detailed line of questioning about your organization. For example:

- Who do they see as your company's top competition for talent, and how are your competitors ranked?

- What three adjectives would they associate with each of the above competitors?
- Specifically, what were the factors that influenced their decision to reject your offer?
  - ▷ What information did they find most useful or surprising along the way?
  - ▷ Would they recommend your company to others, and why/why not?
  - ▷ What is the one thing that your company could have done to cause them to accept the opportunity?

Use the Discussion Guide in the Appendix as a road map.

As with other research, external research can be conducted at any time during the talent branding project. You might consider it after you have put together your brand architecture and creative work to get a real sense of what people will like/dislike/respond to before launching it. Think of it as a studio's sneak-preview screening before releasing a movie. More often than not, the results will justify the costs.

# BUILDING YOUR RESEARCH PLAN

## Building your research plan

If you're unsure about how much or which type of research to include, the questions below can be used as a starting point for thinking about the research plan that's right for you.

**Do we know what current employees think of the employer, and why?**
If you answered no, think about conducting employee surveys and focus groups.

**Do we know what prospective employees outside the organization think of the employer, and why?**
If you answered no, think about conducting external focus groups or interviews.

**Do we know what former employees think of the employer, and why?**
If you answered no, think about conducting interviews or focus groups with former employees you'd like to win back.

**Do we know how we rank versus our direct competitors in the opinions of current, prospective and former employees?**
If you answered no, consider your competition for talent and build this question into your internal/external focus group discussion guide or survey.

**Do we know why employees voluntarily leave?**
If you answered no, think about conducting exit interviews.

**Do we know why prospective employees reject offers?**
If you answered no, think about conducting interviews with candidates.

**Do we know why current employees choose to stay with us?**
If you answered no, include this in your survey or focus group.

**Do we know why prospective employees are attracted to us?**
If you answered no, consider external surveys, or interviews with candidates or recruiters.

**Do we know all of the above for diversity-group candidates or college graduates/MBAs?**
If hiring within these groups is a priority, consider segmenting your external/internal focus groups and surveys.

**Are there any change initiatives pending or under way (mergers, acquisitions, new strategies, downsizing) and do we know what employees think of them?**
If you answered no, include this in your executive interviews or focus group.

# CONDUCTING A COMPETITIVE AUDIT

Competitive differentiation is one of the hallmarks of a great talent brand and, for this reason, you must at some point conduct a competitive audit. This will help you understand the employment marketplace through the eyes of a candidate, and understand what your competition is saying from a talent branding perspective, along with whom they're looking to attract. You'll also get a sense of where the opportunity exists – the space that you must occupy in order to stand out from the competition.

Here are the steps to follow:

**Know your competition** – This may seem like an obvious first step, but let's look a little deeper. If you're an insurance company, your competition would certainly include other insurance companies. But if you're embarking upon a major technology transformation, then the people you're looking to hire might be from tech start-ups, social networks or just about any other non-insurance company you can think of.

So, come up with four or five of your industry competitors. Who do you wish you were, or to whom do you seem to lose your top talent? In fact, ask your star employees, those who you wish you had more of, where they would go if your company didn't exist. If you can, try and come up with additional 'wildcard' competitors, who may not be in your industry, and add them to your list. In total, five or six competitors is a good number to work with.

Now examine the following:

## What are they saying on their careers site?

Do they have a positioning statement, talent brand or EVP? If so, what is it and how much detail do they provide? Have they broken this down into:

- Culture and values?
- Diversity and Inclusion?
- Veteran initiatives?
- Workplace awards?
- Learning and Development?
- Student and graduate initiatives?

## Job opportunities and search engine optimization (SEO)

Take a look at what sorts of jobs they are hiring for and how many positions are posted. Look at how they are promoting themselves and the job opportunities. Take this a step further and do an online search for the job title and the location. Did their job come up on pages 1-3? Now do this for one of your jobs. Did yours pop?

**Rank their career websites against yours, based on these categories:**

- Informative, engaging and up-to-date: Does the site look current? Has it captured your attention?
- Ease of use: Does the site provide easy access to important information without a lot of clicks?
- Personalization: Have they segmented content based on certain audiences, or areas of interest?
- Ease of job search: Do they require candidates to register or have they set up a job alert function? Are there talent communities you can join?
- Interactivity and videos: How many videos are there, and how well are they produced?
- Compare their benefits to those that you offer. How do you stack up?

**– Glassdoor:** Look at their Glassdoor metrics, such as average rating, number of reviews and CEO approval rating. See how you stack up.

**– Social media recruitment:** Which social sites are they using for recruiting and how engaging and frequent are their activities? Analyse their branding and content efforts vs standard job postings and track the likes, shares and comments.

In the end, you should be able to understand the strengths and weaknesses of your own talent branding efforts and gain tremendous insight into where and how you can position yourself to garner an advantage.

# PUTTING IT ALL TOGETHER

This is the information you've been waiting for and is, in a sense, the most difficult to articulate. In this final and most important step of crafting your talent brand, we will examine putting all the research together to create the talent brand architecture. More art than science, this is perhaps the hardest phase in the talent branding process, and one misstep can derail all your efforts up to this point.

Chances are, if you have been the lead in this initiative, you probably have some ideas about what belongs in each section of the talent brand architecture. Put those aside for the moment. **The true objective at this point is to impartially consider all the information you've compiled from your research and put it together in a meaningful way.** While every brand planner has their own tried and true methodology, the following are the steps we use. Feel free to modify this approach in your own way.

1. Print out all your research.

2. Highlight every wonderful, inspirational and aspirational comment you've received.

   In a separate colour, highlight all the comments that represent important considerations. These may be neutral or even negative but will serve as important things to factor in as you put the architecture together.

3. On sticky notes write down every adjective used to describe your culture, the way people feel at work and other descriptive insights you may have collected from your survey and focus groups. Make every effort to combine where similar.

4. Create a spreadsheet. This will be a living document, constantly changing as you or the people involved in this effort come up with new ideas inspired by everything they've heard.

5.  Create two worksheets.
    Call the first 'Talent Brand Architecture' and organize it in seven columns: Talent Brand Vision, Pillar One, Pillar Two, Pillar Three, Pillar Four, EVP and Positioning.
    Call the second 'Talent Brand Data' and set it up in columns to include the specific components collected from your research. This may include:
    *   How we feel working here.
    *   Words that describe our culture.
    *   Important things of note.
    *   Attributes of people who succeed.
    *   People who won't do well.
    *   Our tone of voice.
    *   How we look.

**Now you can start creating your talent brand architecture.**

**Begin by articulating your Talent Brand Vision:**
This will answer the question, "What are we all doing here?" It will be the highest purpose of the work collectively being done by everyone everywhere.

**Once that is complete, begin to assemble the Culture Pillars:**
As the talent brand vision answers the question, "What are we all doing here?", the pillars answer the questions, "How are we doing it?" or "What really makes our company culture unique?"

You may have heard that the one thing that differentiates your culture is your focus on professional development – you are looking for people who will come, stay, grow and build their careers with you. Turn this concept into a pillar and call it 'For the Long Term'. Now, take a look at your talent brand data and see which words and phrases might fall under this pillar. Maybe you have words to work with like stable, sustainable, relationships, learning and development, tenure and growth. Assemble these notes and the direct quotes from the research that supports this pillar. These are your proof points.

**Sub-themes:**
As you go through the research, you will have certain sentiments that cross over various pillars, or are pervasive. Consider these sub-themes and place them underneath the pillars and over the talent brand vision.

Add columns to your spreadsheet as you go along to make sure you capture all the larger themes. Perhaps include your corporate vision, values and consumer brand positioning at the base of your talent brand architecture, directly below your Talent Brand Vision. This will be helpful information to consider as you look to create brand-alignment.

**Create Your Employer Value Proposition:**
As the Talent Brand Vision answers the question, "What are we all doing here", the EVP tells us the "Why". This is the essence of your employment offering and an emotive description that employees in all areas and capacities can stand behind and support.

It is the reflection of who you are as a company, along with what makes individuals and teams successful. It is important to note that this may never appear anywhere as such, but can provide helpful context for how you shape all communications.

What phrase can you own that will embody your employee experience?

**End With Your Talent Brand Positioning Statement:**
This is the slogan, tagline or strapline that will be used very visibly in all communications, internally and externally. It will help your audience quickly understand who you are, what you stand for and what you do. The positioning statement will evoke your personality to your various audiences. Unlike the EVP, the positioning statement may be frequently modified or adapted to fit within a specific campaign or language. When crafting your positioning statement, think about how you can communicate the driving idea behind your culture and work and state it in as few words as possible.

## Now read from the top down

**Talent Brand Positioning Statement**: Your driving idea.
**Employer Value Proposition**: Why you do what you do; What you stand for.
**Pillars**: How you do what you do; What makes you different.
**Talent Brand Vision**: What you're all doing together.
**Sub-themes**: The unifiers across all pillars and positioning.

**How do you know if you've been successful? Make sure you can check every box:**

- Is it authentic?
- Is it differentiated?
- Is it representative of your organization at the highest level?
- Does it have brand-business alignment?
- And finally (and most importantly): Is it emotive?

Look at your worksheet. Have you found a place within your talent brand architecture for all the information you have collected throughout your research and embedded within your Talent Brand data ? If so, at this point you may feel you're in a great place to move forward.

Or you may want to consider getting more help and refinement. Invite more collaboration and consensus-building by holding another stakeholder session, hosting another focus group or conducting another survey. Or you can use an online crowdsourcing tool to see which pillars and statements bubble to the top across the organization.

# SEGMENTATION

Your talent brand architecture needs to be a passionate representation of your organization at its best, and something that all employees can rally around, support and share. But this doesn't mean that everyone everywhere will want, feel and enjoy the same things.

That's why we recommend personalizing your message by audience. This is known as segmentation. Just as consumer branding and marketing allows for different messages based on geography or audience demographics such as gender, education, age and income, so we can build a segmented communication plan that reflects the brand architecture as a foundation, but speaks on a point-wise basis to each slice of your audience.

In building out your segmentation plan, create a column under each pillar for each of your target segments. And then, create supporting messaging and key selling points for each.

To further illustrate, if one of your pillars of differentiation is 'Support for the individual' and your two segments are 'Women' and 'Software engineers', consider how the way in which you go to market might differ based on their unique wants or needs.

Segmentation is not about wavering from your foundational approach to promoting your brand architecture but it does allow you to dial up things that certain subsets of your audience would find desirable.

One segment might find the ability to work from home more appealing while another might want a greater say in what is going on within the office. Or, you may find that there is something desirable about the benefits or office environment in one geographical location. These differences can be woven into your segmented communication plans.

The research methods used to create your brand architecture (internal and external focus groups and surveys, along with your competitive audit) will be very useful in determining more precisely what those appealing, yet non-universal differences might be.

# TALENT BRAND TONE OF VOICE

Part of your talent branding research should include coming to agreement on a unified tone of voice for your communications. Your talent brand voice encompasses the tone of your communications, the style of your content and the personality behind all your writing. A talent brand voice ensures consistency no matter who on your team is creating the content, be it web copy, video scripts, brochures, social posts or emails. Without a strong, intentional voice, your content will sound like a bland corporate press release – or worse, as though your brand has no personality at all.

Within your primary research you should consistently be polling your audiences about the personality you most resemble, which should in turn help determine your talent brand voice.

## Are you a wizard or a warrior?

It may seem difficult to imagine distilling your company's attributes into *a single personality*. But what if I told you that just about every character falls into 1 of 12 categories that symbolize all human motivations?[13]

**For our talent brand research, inspired by the brand archetypes typically associated with consumer branding, we've narrowed it down to just the nine you see below.**

## What's Your Brand Voice?

| The Regular Guy/Gal: Humble, hardworking, and friendly | The Partner: Being in a relationship with the people, work and surroundings they love | The Caregiver: Protecting and caring for others |
| --- | --- | --- |
| The Sage: Using intelligence and analysis to understand the world | The Ruler: Leading people through confidence, determination, and influence | The Revolutionary: Committed to overturning what isn't working |
| The Magician: Making things happen | The Creator: Creating things of enduring value | The Hero: Using expert mastery in a way that improves the world |

Maybe your brand is The Regular Guy/Gal – humble, hard-working and friendly. Or maybe your brand is The Revolutionary – disruptive, rebellious and committed to overturning what isn't working. Or, perhaps, you identify as The Magician – making things happen.

Once you have determined the talent brand archetype, you'll be able to shape the way you communicate with your target audiences. It will also influence the type of information you'd like to share.

13  "The 12 Common Archetypes," Accessed June, 2017,
     http://www.soulcraft.co/essays/the_12_common_archetypes.html/

# VISUAL
# IDENTITY
# DEVELOPMENT

A very important component of your branding success is the development of a recognizable visual identity system. This is the look and feel of your talent brand. We call it a system because it's composed of several visual elements such as logo, colour palette, icons, photos and other imagery and treatments that work together to create a distinct yet cohesive look and feel.

Based on your corporate identity and enhanced through research, your talent brand visual identity will align with the unique qualities of your brand voice and, through repeated use over time, help build a recognizable framework for all employee communications.

Are you going for a warm and inviting approach or more of a bold tone? Is your talent brand aiming to be trendy, disruptive or warm and friendly? Are you part of a conservative financial institution or a dynamic web start-up?

This is where all your research will come into play.

**Align with your corporate brand identity** – Your organization may already have brand guidelines, fonts, imagery and a colour palette, but you may be able to create a secondary palette that, in the future, will only be associated with your talent brand.

**Separate yourself from the competition** – Review the information collected during your competitive audit and consider what options might set you apart from the pack.

**Appeal to the people you need to reach** – If you look at a series of magazine covers, you'll notice that design has changed through the years. How well does your design direction relate to the people you want to reach, here and now?

**Bring your words to life** – In your research you compiled a series of adjectives that describe your company. Now think about imagery that corresponds to those words. Are you quirky, country or cutting-edge? Ask stakeholders to browse through stock photography or consumer magazines and bring in images that they feel represent your talent brand.

**Remain consistent with your talent brand architecture** – Is one of your pillars teamwork? If so, make sure that all your images are of people working together. Do you have a formal dress code or allow employees to bring dogs to work? All of these cultural considerations should inform your identity.

**Which elements are fixed and which can be replaced to allow for regional and global personalization?** Should the logo always be in the lower left corner? Are the colours always the same? While you should allow for a certain amount of individualization and interpretation, be consistent about which things can be changed and which are inherent to your visual identity system.

# TESTING
## 1, 2, 3

It is not unusual for stakeholders to fall in love with their own talent branding efforts and the resulting creative output, particularly if this is the first time they've gone through a talent branding initiative. That's why it's vitally important, before any roadshows, town halls or internal/external reveals, to run tests. Testing will present you with the unbiased feedback you'll want to secure before any large-scale reveal.

Testing can start as early as the architecture/data pillars and creative conception phase to ensure that you're matching your efforts to the user experience.

Test results can be quite surprising. Phrases that you may think make you sound cool, connected or confident might be an unexpected turn-off and have a completely opposite effect from what you intend. I remember hosting a focus group with recent college graduates where the recruitment marketing concepts presented were thought to be incredibly persuasive in generating interest in the client's career opportunities. We were testing against a variety of elements, which included imagery, messaging and benefits. The results were not at all what we expected. We expected participants to be swayed by the opportunity to join a start-up organization and be further impressed by the chance to work remotely, but the results showed that none of this was as appealing as we had thought it would be.

If you're testing participants for their overall reactions, a starting point to generate good group insights might be questions like, "How does this make you feel about working here?" or "What stands out in a positive way?"

Ask if they think that the concepts stand out from the competition and, if not, what changes they'd recommend. If you're presenting multiple concepts, ask participants to list them in the order they find most appealing.

Ask the group to write down their specific dislikes, and what they think about your choice of words, images and pictures, as well as how they are arranged on the page.

When undertaking website testing, sit back and watch how people interact with the site. Watch what they click on first, second and third, and ask why they made those choices.

Ask general questions, like what they might expect to find on specific pages, and if anything is missing or doesn't make sense. Words, acronyms or job titles that may be common in your organization may not be as readily understood on the outside.

As with all our other research, testing can be done with current employees, or potential candidates for areas where you might be looking to hire.

One final note: this may seem obvious, but make sure you're testing with the right group of people. If you're looking to recruit a particular age group, those with certain specialized skills or professionals with long tenure in your field, invite people to participate who represent the target segment. Only then will you be guaranteed a true picture of what works with whom.

# CREATING A BRAND BOOK

A good brand book will help you improve the efficiency and effectiveness of your communications by fostering increased cohesion among employees. It arms management with all the information they need to create compelling, memorable and easy-to-use HR communications. The effect on the organization's culture is profound; in some cases, a strong communications brand book really can save a culture from apathy, low morale or competing visions.

Begin by collecting all your brand voice information and some sample content into a book format. Include any relevant content information; if you refer to customers as 'guests' (as the Disney parks do), put it in the book. Include identity guidelines, to make sure your website, mobile site, affiliate sites, social channels, press materials and marketing deliverables all look the same. Distribute the book to anyone who might create (or approve) content. Treat this as a living document that reflects changes in your organization as new terms, new products or new audiences are reached out to.

You can also bring all content developers together for a workshop that walks them through the tone of voice and illustrates the difference between 'on-brand' and 'off-brand' words, phrases and information suitable for sharing and dissemination.

**Here are some generic attributes that can be included in your talent brand book:**

### Overview of the brand

An employee can't write something that aligns with the organization's brand if they don't know what it is! The first part of any brand book should include the company's mission, vision and values, as well as a detailed explanation of your talent brand and architecture and how they intersect.

### Additional sections

- General design guidelines that explain the unifying characteristics of all talent communications.
- Logo guidelines, with approved and unapproved examples.
- Colour palette, with official Pantone colours for print work and their web equivalents.
- Typography, listing the organization's official fonts.
- Imagery guidelines, covering things like the use of photos of actual employees vs stock photography.

### Samples

As clear as a brand book's instructions may be, nothing beats seeing actual examples. The last part of the book should include images and templates for every type of communication, from employee newsletters to recruitment materials to digital assets.

# YOUR TALENT BRAND MANIFESTO

This piece is the purposeful, inspiring summary statement that ties together all the elements of your talent brand architecture. With typically no more than four or five paragraphs on a page, the manifesto will energize people about your company, its culture and the purpose of their work.

While creating the manifesto is not necessarily easy, it is probably one of my favourite outputs of the talent branding process since it pulls together all of the work you and the team have laboured through and showcases it in one place.

To create the manifesto, collect your spreadsheet and all of the sticky notes used to create your talent brand architecture and all the wonderful and deeply moving phrases you've captured from your research.

You might start your writing with your EVP at the top of the page, and follow with three simple words:

"At (company name), we…"

From there, you can begin working on who you are, what you are attempting to achieve, or things you collectively believe. Prepare some content inspired by each of the pillars and use as many of the words you've amassed on the stickies and your spreadsheet as you can.

End your manifesto with your talent brand vision statement and what is important about the work you're doing.

As you re-read what you've created, consider the following:

## Is it inspiring?

Would you be proud to read it on your careers page, or hand it out at a recruiting fair or employee event?

## Is it aligned with your talent brand tone of voice?

Imagine a celebrity brand spokesperson reading it as the voiceover to a video. How well does it work?

## Is it emotive?

The manifesto might make you laugh or cry but it should always make you proud to work for your organization.

# BRIEFLY ON
# THE BRIEFS

Within this book I have tried to provide you with all the resources you'll need to successfully manage your talent branding initiatives, and as such there are a number of in-house agency tools you'll find useful. Most notable are the briefs.

Briefs serve a great purpose and are the starting point for every new client and project. Not only do they offer a great way to consider and agree upon the goals and objectives at the start of each project, but they also provide a checklist of considerations you'll need to think about on order to be as efficient as possible with your manpower and finances.

In using the brief, the assumption is made that internal and external partners will be constantly changing as new people come and go. Therefore, when filling out the brief, it is critical that you are as specific as possible so that anyone coming in will have a complete understanding of the objectives, elements and desired outcomes for the overall project and each piece of it.

If it is your talent branding brief, consider such factors as the goals of the project, your target audience, the resources you currently have and how your success will be measured.

If it is a social media brief, start with thinking about what you're truly looking to achieve via your social efforts. That in turn might influence your choice of social activities, outlets and the metrics used to gauge success.

Is it a creative brief that you will be sharing with internal marketing partners, or external agency partners? Make sure you think about the assets you have and the corporate identity that's already in place.

## File Formats

Another important and often overlooked consideration for every project is the file formats you'd like. Are you creating something that will be frequently changed, and if so will you want to make those changes yourself? If the answer is yes and it's a website, you'll want to make certain you build a content marketing system (CMS) into the project plan. If it's a PowerPoint, make sure that you create a template so that the file can be shared without losing the integrity of the fonts and colours. And if it is a template, make sure that you have tested it on multiple platforms and browsers, with users of various skill levels.

Unfortunately, some of the most beautifully designed pieces of work are created using Adobe Creative Suite programmes such as InDesign, Illustrator and Photoshop. Unless you're a designer or are working with one, these will be the least friendly pieces to change.

The briefs included in the Appendix should be considered a starting point only. Use them, personalize them and enhance them in a way that benefits your particular needs, projects, teams and style of work.

# The Creative Brief

1. Background/Overview: Who we are, and what do we stand for?

2. Objective: What is the goal of the campaign?

3. Target audience: Who are we talking to?

4. Key messages: What is the tone of the messaging?

5. Creative Elements
   - Slogans/taglines?
   - Trademarks?
   - Visuals?
   - Other?

6. Tone and Image
   - Identify the general tone of voice and brand image you want to convey.
   - What do the audiences believe or think, before you start communicating with them?
   - What tone and imagery should you use to engage them?
   - Specific visual goals?
   - If you could get one sentence across, what would that be and what are the proof points?

7. What else might help the creative team?

8. Deliverables/Schedule: What do we need, and when do we need it?

# YOUR WISH LIST OF TALENT BRAND MESSAGING AND TOOLS

With a new talent brand and visual identity, the next step is to make sure the key framework of your talent brand architecture and manifesto is represented in some way within all communications. A recent study we conducted showed that following a talent branding initiative, all the materials below were created and/or changed:

- Social media.
- Careers site.
- Recruitment videos.
- Talent brand guidelines.
- Internal communications.
- Recruitment advertising.
- Recruitment brochures.
- Campus recruiting materials.
- New-hire materials and orientation.
- Job board templates.

Below is a more comprehensive list you can use as a guide, but your own decisions will be influenced by several considerations, including your initial goals and objectives (per your talent branding brief), your communications audit (more on that shortly) and of course your budget.

### Talent acquisition materials:
- Careers site.
- Recruiter toolkit: FAQs, benefits rundown, elevator pitch, emails.
- Talent brand book.
- Campus recruiting.
- Event marketing materials: booth, presentation, brochures, giveaways.
- Recruitment brochure.
- Job board templates.

- Employee day-in-the-life videos.
- Social recruiting.
- Employee referral programme.
- Diversity communications.
- CRM tools and apps.

## Onboarding materials:
- Offer letters.
- Orientation package/meeting.
- Onboarding site.
- New-hire welcome kit.

## Employee engagement materials:
- Culture videos.
- Learning and development materials.
- Intranet.
- Culture book.
- Employee handbook.
- Engagement support.
- Compensation and benefits communications.
- CRM tools and apps.

## Talent management communications:
- Annual Report.
- Corporate Social Responsibility.

# JOURNEY MAPPING

The most strategic way to allocate time and resources to your communications development is to conduct a journey-mapping session.

**Start with your goals. For example:**
- Ease in attracting candidates.

**Then think about your current process for talent acquisition, which might include:**
- Job postings.
- LinkedIn.
- External recruiters.

**These will be the first things that may change. But keep going:**
Now think of all the touchpoints where people intersect the process. How did the candidate get to the job openings? If it was through your careers site, add that to the list. Maybe it was through an employee referral programme. Invite employees who've referred job candidates to your company to become ambassadors and make sure they have access to the most relevant and updated materials to promote your talent brand. Prepare resources, tools or even a microsite where employees can find out more about your talent brand and share the most current information with potential candidates.

Incorporating candidate and employee journey mapping into your communications plan will help ensure that your recruiting partners, employees and potential employees are well informed, and have a wonderful experience with your talent brand wherever they are in their process.

# HOW TO PRIORITIZE THROUGH A COMMUNICATIONS AUDIT

The best way to ensure that your talent brand is clearly communicated in all your employee and recruitment materials is to conduct a communications audit. This is when you collect all the pieces of information currently in use by all departments and analyse them against a set of criteria.

And though it sounds incredibly daunting, don't be threatened by the idea of it. It's not something that will undermine the great job you are already doing as a communications professional. A communications audit will showcase the work you are doing and help you to prioritize the projects you want to focus on. If you are working on a branding or rebranding initiative, this is the perfect time to embark on a communications audit and tie the two activities together.

Read on for communications audit tips, so that you can do your best work yet.

## Set a timeline

Set some deadlines around when you expect to start and end your communications audit, culminating with a target date for presentation of your overall findings. Does it make sense to aim for your mid-year or annual performance review? Should your summary be timed to coincide with a business priority, such as before you begin the annual planning or budget process? You may identify projects that need a complete overhaul and warrant a separate timeline, or certain activities that you think can be stopped at some strategic point and may need wind-down time.

If you have a team, this is the time to engage them in the overall vision for the audit and let them know they will be part of the process – and the decision-making.

Block time on your calendar to work on the audit. Even if it is just an hour a week or part of the time dedicated to your weekly team meetings, dedicating focused time to it will make it feel like the priority it needs to be – but not overwhelming.

## Gather what you have

You have more than you think to get started. Here is a short list of items to start assembling:

- Annual Reports
- Recruitment materials.
- Sales collateral.
- Benefits communications.
- Web publications.
- Print deliverables.
- Communications for specific groups/departments.
- Other HR-oriented communications.

## Dive in

This is where you are going to roll up your sleeves and pull together the details off each item on your list.

You will want to put together a grid for each piece that outlines the following:

- Tone of voice. (Is it effective? How should it evolve?)
- Branding and design. (Does it follow the guidelines? How does it fit with other materials? Does it all work as a campaign?)
- Message consistency.
- Recommendations. (Can the communications be combined with something else? Does it need to change significantly?)
- Channels used and their effectiveness.

- Gap analysis. (What could you have done better? What should you try next time? What audiences were reached effectively? Who wasn't? How can you become more digital?)
- Writing style. (Does it work for our audience? Should it change if the project comes up again?)

## Hold a stakeholder review

This is a good place to do a 'client' or 'stakeholder' review, to evaluate your relationship with those you are creating content for and what feedback you may need to share with them to have an even better outcome next time. Some thought starters:

- Did they clearly articulate their goals and objectives?
- Did they *own* their subject matter and give you the facts/content you needed?
- Did they give you enough lead time?
- Did they meet the review deadlines?
- Did they take the time to review the results?

I know you know this, but before you make a lot of changes run them by whomever you need to – your boss, your boss's boss, etc. Get agreement and have an action plan for going forward. Plot out what you will stop, start and continue, and when you will be talking to your stakeholders.

## What can you stop?

The only way you can go further on your priority projects is to stop doing selected lower-priority work. Use the facts to support that decision. Find ways to combine or streamline messages. Or maybe it just means YOU need to stop doing it – but it's a great learning opportunity for someone on your team.

## Where do you need to go, to go further?

For campaigns that need a revamp, you'll need to set aside time separate from your communications audit to evaluate how you will make these projects sing through the channel, voice, tone, branding, design or writing changes and where they fall on the list of priorities. This is a great opportunity to look at the workload of your team and redistribute work so that high-potential team members have stretch opportunities or the visibility they (or you!) need.

# YOUR
# CAREERS
# SITE

An organization's careers site is typically the first outward evidence of their talent branding efforts. A digital experience may ultimately be the deciding factor that compels your ideal candidate to click that 'apply' button with confidence. And while all that glitters isn't gold, your most important recruiting asset is potentially your careers site, so here are some simple steps to make sure it's effective, efficient and aesthetically pleasing.

## Be mission-driven

Without a doubt, your careers site should have the ability to answer questions like, "What will inspire me to come to work every day?' and "Why should I choose to join this particular organization?"

Creating a careers site that is beyond a job listing means that you must adapt and learn how to speak to today's top talent. Modern-day candidates are eager to make their mark on the world, create a profound difference, and contribute to a greater vision. They are motivated by more than money – they want depth, meaning and purpose, and are placing an increasing emphasis on joining mission-driven organizations. They want to be emotionally connected to their position and the company that they choose to work for.

Does your careers site convey your talent brand vision? Do you display how your employees feel about their work? Most importantly, does it share what it means to be a part of your organization?

## Embody your employer value proposition, lead with your corporate culture

Let's face it, content is king and visuals are an increasingly influential aspect of talent branding. A combination of fresh copy and compelling visuals will tell your story through the perspective of your team and showcase the daily life of the office. Showing a passionate and enthusiastic company culture creates a strong connection with potential candidates.

## Let your team speak for itself

A picture is worth a thousand words. Put your employees at the forefront; they are after all the heart and soul of the organization. If a benefit of working for your company is that it is highly team-oriented, prove it. Using eye-catching visuals that showcase your environment, culture and team interaction will increase the impact and credibility of your careers site. This will compel potential candidates in a way that even the most extensive text cannot. Those who are eager to build lasting relationships with a team committed to a common goal are motivated by seeing real employees, real environments and real opportunities.

# The Careers Site Brief

## Website Creative/Technology Brief

- What is the URL of the site?

- What are your two or three most important goals for the site?

- Who are the primary audiences for the site?

- What would they be most interested in knowing about your company?

- What do you want them to think or do after having visited your site?

- How will you measure the success of your site?

- Who will maintain the finished site?

- Which websites do you like; which do you dislike?

- Do you have an EVP?

- What makes you better than your competition?

- Circle any of the following terms that apply to your vision for your site: informative, lucrative, attractive, serene, honest, mature, family, scholarly, educational, useful, popular, clean, colourful, whimsical, humorous, serious, profitable, unusual, cosy, clear-cut, warm and fuzzy, supportive, innovative, fast-moving.

- Do you have design elements in mind that portray these terms to you and your visitors?

- Do you have any custom graphic needs or will you be able to supply all of the images required?

- Do you have any 'must haves' or 'must not haves' for the site (mobile, video, discussion, social integration, etc.)?

**Production**
- How many pages will the site contain and what are the headers?

- What special technical or functional requirements are needed?

- What is the budget for the site?

- What is the production schedule for the site, including intermediate milestones and dates?

- Who are the people on the project team and what are their responsibilities?

- What type of security is required for the site? Will there be sensitive files that need to be protected?

- Do you need a password-protected site?

- What are the SEO considerations you'll need to work through to make your site search-engine friendly?

Identify your top-ten keywords and your top-ten key phrases – the words and phrases that search engines may use to locate your site in response to an inquiry.

To rank well with search engines, your site should contain quality content, using the actual words and phrases your prospects are searching with. These keywords will need to be used in the text of your pages, so it is important to select them carefully.

# PART 3

# ACTIVATE YOUR TALENT BRAND INTERNALLY

# CREATING INTERNAL TALENT BRAND AMBASSADORS

You've done it. You have a stellar talent brand. Your careers website tells the story you need to convey – about your culture, the talent you are seeking and the opportunities you have for those who are a 'culture add' rather than simply a 'culture fit'. You're getting résumés from the right candidates for the right jobs. Things couldn't be better.

But aren't you forgetting something? Once your exciting new candidates have become new employees, is your talent brand holding up internally? And, just as importantly, do your existing employees feel like they are a part of the story?

## Where to begin

Now is the time to take the principles of your talent brand and make sure it applies internally across all your communications points of contact, from your intranet to your training programmes. Here are some tips on where to begin.

## Create internal awareness of your talent brand

As you developed your talent brand, it is likely that you shared it with and sought input and approval from your senior leaders, key HR stakeholders, your communications teams and hopefully some influential managers. Now it is time to go further. Consider hosting a Town Hall or holding an all-hands meeting or webinar. Create an overview presentation of your talent brand and what it conveys relative to your culture and employment with the company. An appropriate time to launch might be in conjunction with a milestone of your performance management cycle, merit increases or bonus payouts, or when the company releases its yearly goals or strategy.

Once you have communicated your talent brand to employees, get them involved. And I don't mean just through your employee referral programme. Consider tactics such as having employees create personal statements (with photos). For instance, "I'm proud to work for my company because..." or "I enjoy coming to work every day because..." Have them share these affirmations on your intranet or internal social media channels. Consider partnering with your external communications teams to share the best ones on your corporate social media channels to further your corporate reputation and talent brand.

## Consider the employee experience

Will the candidate experience be consistent with the employee experience? Are various touch points across the employee life cycle telling the same story as your talent brand? Is your talent brand coming through in your internal communications?

Take the time to look at some of your internal processes to ensure that they are reinforcing your talent brand and that your new hires and existing employees hear the story that is being told externally.

**Some key areas that may need updating or refreshing include:**
- New hiring onboarding and orientation.
- Learning and development programmes/training – especially training for new people managers, inclusion and diversity seminars, rollouts of the code of conduct, etc.
- Performance management process. Did you promise ongoing feedback during the hiring process and are you living up to it? Are your people managers equipped to do it?
- Talent management and succession planning. Are you honouring the tenets of your talent brand as you evaluate the organization's future talent plans?

If you haven't yet conducted your Communications Audit, review all of your internal materials from top to bottom – from new hire paperwork to benefits brochures, to your intranet platform, to signage around the office. Does everything support the talent you want to keep today and the talent you want to inspire tomorrow? Each piece of internal communications should support the story you want to tell about who you are as an employer dedicated to attracting new talent and keeping your best talent.

# IS YOUR MESSAGE GETTING THROUGH TO REMOTE EMPLOYEES?

With the influx of millennials and an emphasis on work-life balance, remote workers are becoming an increasingly vital segment of the workforce. So, lets delve into strategies for reaching and engaging all the segments of a staff.

## First, make sure everyone knows they are included

According to an *Inc.* magazine article,[14] one difficult aspect of managing remote workers is how to loop them in. Be sure to include everyone in meetings (using videos, your intranet or a conduit like GoToMeeting), and publicly acknowledge contributions of remote workers. Take steps to keep them informed of what's going on back at the office, especially when it comes to epic staff events such as an audit, benefits open enrolment, or employee milestones and achievements.

## Next, launch an enlightened internal communications plan

A solid internal communications plan captures attention and bolsters employee engagement. Today's plans are increasingly social and interactive, enabling real-time conversations between office-based and remote staff members. The savviest companies communicate with a multi-channel approach to advertising and marketing, and that model is equally important when broadcasting messages inside the company.

---

14   "6 Ways to Keep Your Remote Workers Engaged and Productive," Accessed July, 2017, https://www.inc.com/minda-zetlin/what-do-remote-workers-do-all-day-6-ways-to-keep-them-engaged-and-productive.html

## Use your intranet, blog and social media

From sharp videos to updates on your blog or Facebook pages, internal information can be made into something that is compelling and memorable. Use posts to remind people of upcoming deadlines, new bids/projects, or an ongoing employee referral programme. Celebrate social events like weddings, new hires and promotions, or the team that ran that half-marathon.

## Create a buddy system

Remember as a child when you were paired with a buddy for school trips or summer camp? The 'Accountability Partners' strategy pairs different workers in different locations to ensure that they stay on track. From checking in on a project's status to asking probing questions, buddying-up works to everyone's advantage. I learned of this concept from Freelancers Union, America's largest collective of remote workers.

## Brainstorm

The best way to make sure your messages are hitting their mark is to create remote ambassadors who can let you know whether your story is getting through and come up with ideas on how to improve your cascade. Thinking about creative solutions is a great way to unite people in different locales.

# PART 4

# ACTIVATE YOUR TALENT BRAND EXTERNALLY

# THE TALENT BRANDING GUIDE TO BLOGGING

Think of your company's talent blog as the key to displaying your company culture, increasing your brand awareness, driving traffic and conversions, and enhancing your candidate experience. Potential candidates are checking you out on Google and Glassdoor before they even think to visit your careers site. A talent blog gives you and your employees the power to influence how your company is perceived as an employer by building an authentic brand story from multiple contributors.

Follow these simple steps to create compelling content that will keep your audience coming back for more.

## Know your reader

Having a clear idea of who you are creating content for is a crucial aspect of creating branded content that will resonate. Once you have established your target audience, that will lead to repeat visits, word-of-mouth recommendations and the attraction of new readers and leads. Create consistent content that is helpful to your reader, covering topics and answering questions that are tailored to their needs. You can easily establish your credibility and authority by addressing topics that are not only company-centric, but audience-centric as well.

## Personalize your communication

Impactful content will give your audience the opportunity to get an inside look at your culture, gain a feel for the work environment, see your team in action and see you in your element as a leader within your industry. As a valuable voice of your brand, your employees can be transformed into brand ambassadors when given the chance to express their unique knowledge and experience on your blog. Including your team in the content creation process empowers them, grants them ownership, provides diversity in brand perspective and reinforces the overall brand message. Best of all, it can help them build their personal brand as well. All told, it's a win-win proposition.

## Create a call to action

I know what you're probably thinking: How does a blog post lead to candidate conversions? The answer is simple. Think of every new blog post as an opportunity to generate a new lead, to tee up a new potential employee. For every blog post that's created, another indexed page is added to your website, instantly augmenting your SEO. Consistent content creation – with a call to action – drives traffic to your website, leading to an organic search and the possibility of a conversion. Whether it's a continuation of the topic at hand or an invitation to join your talent community, a click-worthy call to action will entice visitors to click through to an additional landing page.

## Be authentic and consistent

It's simple: be personable and dependable. You'll be surprised at how much your readers will appreciate it. Spend time creating content that is worth reading and build your content calendar. In order to get the ball rolling, map out your topics of focus, be realistic about how frequently you can post and how much time you can invest in the creative process, and execute when time and marketing support allow. Be sure that you share this engaging content across multiple social media channels, like Facebook, Twitter and LinkedIn. To up the ante, construct your blog in such a way that readers can easily share the content and subscribe for future content, to stay updated on your organization and its activities.

**Now that you have a handle on these go-to steps, start blogging with these potential topics in mind:**

1. How-to guides.
2. Employee testimonials and spotlights.
3. Helpful tips and tricks.
4. Recognition received or awards won.
5. Leadership team interviews.
6. New ventures or partnerships.
7. Company milestones or anniversaries.
8. Executive speaking engagement announcements.
9. Consumer testimonials or success stories.
10. Market research about your industry.
11. Trends that affect your industry.
12. Company events and a behind-the-scenes look at the organization.

With consistent effort and precise execution, blogging can play a pivotal role in your overall marketing strategy, allowing you to enhance your brand-building efforts, manage your reputation, stand tall against your competitors and engage with your target demographic. This is your chance to amplify your internal branding and drive retention, all the while attracting and influencing your ideal talent.

# THE RECIPE FOR A SUCCESSFUL EMPLOYMENT VIDEO

Video content is crucial to your talent branding and content marketing success. Compelling, well-produced videos enhance your employer profile, recruiting, search engine optimization and candidate experience.

Create a targeted approach for sharing unique differentiators, your organization's point of view and the culture of the work environment. Use the power of persuasion to create a personal connection, and bring it to life with the help of widely available multimedia tools and capabilities. Specialized external vendors can be retained to help with this.

## Solidify your messaging and company culture

Is your target audience internal, external, or both? Always keep your talent branding message in mind and ensure that it is segmented toward the correct audience. One message may not satisfy all. Once you identify your target audience, you will understand exactly the type of content that will resonate best with them. Talent branding videos that present a realistic look at your culture help keep your internal audience involved and inspired, while giving your external audience a closer look at what your organization has to offer.

## Bring your mission to life

Attract the best and brightest by telling your brand story in a compelling way that words alone can't convey. Talent branding is about making an impact, and videos are one of the most efficient ways to spread a powerful message. Share the culture that shapes the minds of the team by conveying your brand values, the potential for career growth and exactly what it means to be a part of your organization.

## Improve your SEO

Videos appear in 70% of the top-100 search listings, and they're 53 times more likely than text to show up on the first page of search results.[15] The number of job-related searches is increasing by the minute, and your goal should be to land the top spot within your candidates' search engine results. Now is the time to increase your digital presence, enhance your search visibility strategy, and optimize your website and content for search results across all channels. After all, if no one is seeing the content that you worked so hard to create, how will they discover how great you are?

For organizations that have an employee referral programme in place, shareable videos can be distributed to your team's entire network with the click of a button. The more shareable content that you create, the more shares, views and positive word-of-mouth buzz you'll generate.

## Let your employees shine

A sure-fire way to attract potential candidates with a similar work ethic, passion and outlook is to put your team at the forefront. Employee video testimonials are a genuine representation of your organization's work style, highlighting the range of roles and sharing the brand story through the eyes of the team members themselves. Beyond showing the diversity of the team, employee testimonials spotlight the qualities and traits they have in common, whether it is fearlessness, inventiveness or adaptability.

---

15  "The SEO Secret Weapon," Accessed June, 2017,
http://www.business2community.com/seo/the-seo-secret-weapon-video-0378444#F3JuoF11pDmBSy75.97/

Your ideal candidate will appreciate the human connection you've created. Giving your candidates the best understanding of what they should expect from you (and vice versa) can help reduce employee turnover. After reviewing your multimedia, they will have a better sense of their cultural fit, your team dynamic and the legacy you can build together.

Here are some final hints:

- **Content**

  Like most other content and entertainment, the videos that do best are those that evoke an emotional response. The key is to determine which style best matches your brand voice. Are you a 'fun' organization? A 'serious' one? An innovator, a legacy, a start-up? Your videos should fit into your current marketing and recruiting campaigns, which reflect your company's mission, vision and values.

- **Production**

  Poor quality can kill the best-written or best-edited video. Make sure you have good lighting, whether that means turning on all the overheads, opening your curtains, or renting actual studio lights. Sound is also important, and a camera phone doesn't always capture it well. Luckily, there are plenty of smartphone audio accessories that will provide stereo playback. You can also rent a camera with a good microphone, or a boom mic, or clip-on microphones.

- **Post-production**

  Add titles, graphics, music and sound effects to make your video look and sound truly professional. Look online for sources of free images and music. The more polish you can give to your videos, the more they'll stand out from the crowd.

- **Length**

  The average length of YouTube's 50 most popular videos is **just under three minutes**. The 50 most shared videos clock in at the same length. Makes sense; that's about the length of a pop song or a movie trailer. Then again, a study by Visible Measures found that 60% of viewers stop watching a video by the two-minute mark. This is one instance where shorter can be better.

# The Video Brief

1. **Purpose**
   What are your two or three most important goals for the video?

2. **Target audience**
   Who do you want to watch your video? Can they be characterized in any way? What do they already know about the your company? What sort of things will appeal to them?

3. **Distribution**
   Where will your video be shown or watched? Will you be using it on the web, on a DVD, in a presentation, looped on a monitor at a trade show?

4. **Content**
   What are the key messages that the video has to communicate? Is there a secondary use for this material? What do you want your viewers to think after watching the video? How do you want viewers to feel when they watch your video?

5. **Narration**
   Do you want your video to have voice-over narration? Would you like a professional voice-over, or a presenter to lead the video?

6. **Style**
   Have you seen any particular videos that you liked? (If so, make a list of them.)

7. **Image**
   How does the company want its image to be perceived?

8. **Circle any of the following terms that apply to your vision of your video**
   Friendly, elite, intimate, informative, lucrative, attractive, serene, honest, mature, family, scholarly, educational, useful, popular, clean, colourful, edgy, whimsical, humorous, serious, profitable, unusual, cosy, clear-cut, warm and fuzzy, supportive, innovative, fast-moving.

9. **Corporate identity**
   Are there corporate standards we should know about? (Supply information regarding logo restrictions, colours, fonts, design guidelines, etc.)

10. **Locations**
    How many locations will be used for filming? (Make a list of them.) Are they indoor, outdoor, or both?

11. **Talent**
    How many subjects will be interviewed? Will you require professional hair/make-up services?

12. **Basic requirements**
    Do you have any 'must-haves' or 'must-not-haves' for the video?

13. **Your deadline**
    When must the video be completed? Are there any important dates/events around which the production must be scheduled?

## 14. Production

- How long will the final video be?

- Will it be scripted?

- Are there special technical or functional requirements?

- Do you have any music requirements?

- What is the budget for the video?

- Who are the people on the video project team and what are their responsibilities?

- Do you have any custom graphics or special effects needs?

### Video Testimonial Script

Subject talking points – recruiting / onboarding videos:

- What compelled you to want to work here?

- What is your favourite thing about working here?

- Tell me a little bit about the culture – friendly, work hard/play hard, team-oriented, corporate, stable?

- What types of people succeed here?

- How do you feel about your opportunities for growth within the company?

- How is this job different from others you've had?

- What do you wish you'd known before you started?

- What surprised you the most when you got here?

- Would you recommend this company as a great place to work? If so, why?

- If a friend were interested in working here, what would you tell them?

- What piece of advice would you give to someone on their first day?

- Are you involved through the company in any charities/community events?

- How is the work/life balance?

- Do you feel this job has helped you to achieve any of your personal hopes and dreams?

- Do you feel you can make a difference in your work? If so, how?

- What was your proudest moment?

- What are you looking forward to next?

# SOCIALIZE YOUR TALENT BRAND WITH AN EMPLOYEE REFERRAL PROGRAMME

The data speaks for itself. According to multiple studies and surveys, employee referral programmes are the number-one source of hire.[16] And their brilliance as a tool for sharing your talent brand is that they're social in nature, are activated internally (from your employees), are externally facing (via their social networks), and they're typically lots of fun.

Here are the fundamentals for building a successful employee referral programme.

## Determine the who, what and when

Start with the basics: Who owns the programme? Ideally, the team would include someone from recruiting, someone from compensation and benefits, and someone from internal communications, since all three forms of expertise play into this sort of programme. The other 'who' to think about is who are you looking for? Which sorts of employees for which departments? When will the programme begin and end? If you need to fill 50 IT positions in 6 months, your strategy will look quite different from the one that seeks 100 salespeople in 6 weeks.

Also consider small details such as eligibility, how and when the awards will be paid (tax-free, charitable donations, presented with fanfare) and a process for recruitment-bonus dispute resolution.

---

16   "2017 Sources of Hire Report," ( June 2017).
      http://blog.silkroad.com/index.php/2017/05/2017-sources-of-hire-report/

## Create the communications

Your employees have to know the rules and the benefits of the programme in order to take part in it. You'll need a catchy name with a fun slogan that conveys your talent brand. The design and copy that conveys this information should reflect your campaign theme, with an emphasis on all the content you've recently created that's now part of your talent brand toolkit.

This extends to the supporting materials you'll provide to employees, such as virtual badges for the social media profiles, short links to share on Twitter, or physical handouts to give to their friends. Be sure to display reminders, milestones, deadlines – and, of course, winners – in the workplace and on your intranet.

Along with social media outlets, other methods of communicating include:

- Emails (directly from senior executives).
- Branded newsletters.
- Competitions and events.
- Partnerships with employee resource groups.
- Posters/signage/screensavers.

## Make it fun

Gaming adds another level of competition and engagement to employee referral programmes by allowing employees within various departments, locations or business units to compare their efforts against one another. Leaderboards and live scoring keep employees continuously engaged in the programme and help generate better results. You may want to send a weekly email that shows the programme's progress and identifies both winners and new hires.

## Choose prizes that employees will value

You could save thousands of dollars in hiring costs through an employee referral programme, so you can afford give more than a $25 gift card as a prize. In industries such as technology and healthcare, I've heard of employee referral bonuses that go as high as $20,000 for certain high-profile positions. However, the typical range is between $1,000 and $5,000 for full-time, non-exempt positions.

## Non-monetary prizes are also appealing

If you can't award large payouts or flashy prizes, there are plenty of low-cost alternatives, such as a premium parking space, lunch with the CEO or extra vacation time. No matter the prize, make the employee who gets involved feel special and appreciated, which helps not only the ERP but your organization's morale as well. Publicize the winners through every internal channel so that other employees will want to redouble their efforts. And don't forget to honour the new hire as well!

You can also consider extending referral bonus opportunities to people outside your organization. This is known as an external referral bonus. While there are certain considerations, such as taxes and payroll issues, this is also a growing trend.

## Learn the latest techniques

Use technology to manage your employee referral programme and make it easy to post opportunities, measure response, keep track of candidates and prizes and, most importantly, let employees know where their candidates are in the pipeline. There are a number of third-party technology providers who can help you manage this, but you can also consider the option of building your own ERP management system.

## Ask for help if you need it

If you're aware of critical new business initiatives, expansion plans or anything that will increase hiring, make sure to bring employees, vendors, recruiters and other external partners into the fold as soon as possible.

An employee referral programme is a fantastic way to socialize your talent brand and find talent that fits your culture and strengthens your engagement with current workers. It decreases cost-per-hire, time-to-hire and turnover.

Your ideal process could look something like this:

Step 1: Define your:
- Talent brand.
- Programme stakeholders/administrators.
- Programme scope, roles, geographic reach.
- Rewards, timing.
- Metrics.

Step 2: Get senior leaders involved.

Step 3: Create talent brand ERP identity and materials.

Step 4: Plan internal and external activation strategies and events.

Step 5: Compile and analyse the results.

# OPERATIONALIZE YOUR TALENT BRAND

The way in which you attract, hire and onboard candidates will be the first series of challenges in building an authentic talent brand.

Here are some things to think about as you go through the process.

## Talent branding and your job postings

While you may be legally required to include certain details in job postings, this shouldn't discourage you from creatively embedding elements of your talent brand architecture into these listings. Think about beginning with your manifesto and adding the job title afterward. Leverage your tone of voice as you build brand awareness.

There are no positions too small or insignificant to prevent you from making them shine. If, in the past, you've hired a receptionist, you might have listed the responsibilities as answering phones, greeting visitors and sorting mail. But instead, what if you said, "This is a significant opportunity for you to showcase our culture and become the face and voice of our brand." What kind of up-front impression would that make on jobseekers?

## On-brand applications, rejections and the interview process

Simple things can make a difference, such as responding to emails, providing one point of contact, giving someone your undivided attention during an interview, and providing them with written information in advance to let them know what they can expect when they show up for the interview.

Think back to your talent brand research. What types of people do well within your culture? Are they curious, energetic or passionate about your mission? What kinds of questions can you include that not only help you decide whether they're right for the role, but also help them decide whether it's right for them?

For instance, Zappos asks people to rate, on a scale of 1-10, how lucky they consider themselves. This is because studies show that people who consider themselves lucky are also inclined to think 'out of the box', and that's who does well in the online shoe retailer's culture.

The ride-hailing service Uber has been known to pick people up in an Uber car and interview them while on the road.

Invite candidates to share materials beyond résumés and work portfolios – perhaps something they created, like a painting, a photograph or a video. How much could a recruiter learn about someone if they were asked to bring in something that means a lot to them on a personal level? Would that help show off their personality?

Customize your applications to reflect your company's mission, vision and values, and ask questions that help determine a good culture fit.

- If your cultural pillars reflect the organization's commitment and caring, react in kind to an applicant's interest in the opportunities you provide. Respond in a timely manner to applications; don't leave candidates waiting for their interviews. Create a process of interviewing and rejection that lets prospects know you care about them already. If the candidate is rejected, offer constructive feedback via email.

- Embed your brand into your offer letters and benefits packages. Make sure that once an offer is accepted, an incoming employee knows about your ERP. Remember, as soon as they give notice to their previous employer, they're in a position to bring their best co-workers with them. There is nothing more powerful than FOMO (fear of missing out).

## On-brand new employee orientation

Make sure you are ready for your new arrivals with everything they need, including business cards, phones, computers and branded swag. Show them around the workplace and introduce them to your brand ambassadors, thought leaders and executives. Encourage them to share their new opportunity and initial experiences on their social pages and employment-related sites like Glassdoor. And, give them an immersive opportunity to participate in talent branding early on.

# BUILDING SOCIAL RELATIONSHIPS

## The four stages of social media marketing for talent branding

The effect that social media has on branding strategy is undeniable. Some 71% of consumers who have had a good social media service experience with a brand are likely to recommend it to others. These days, job candidates research potential employers in the same way they do the products and services that they want to buy. Let's be honest, a prospective candidate is more likely to visit your Facebook, Glassdoor or Instagram page before your website to get a better understanding of your marketing aesthetic, corporate culture and work environment. A thoughtful, well-balanced social media campaign can allow you to control how your talent brand is presented. Social media marketing should go hand-in-hand with branding, digital marketing, advertising and corporate communications efforts to highlight your employer value proposition.

1. **Create a social strategy**

   Don't limit your reach by only focusing on one platform. Growing your company's presence on platforms like Facebook, LinkedIn, Twitter, Snapchat, Instagram, Pinterest and Google+ can transform your fans into followers and applicants. Different companies in different industries have different objectives, meaning that your aim for each channel may not be the same. Whether your ultimate goal is to generate more leads through your site, pump newsletter subscriptions or maximize webinar registrations, your aim should always be to foster relationships with current and future employees.

2. **Characterize your current and prospective target audiences**

   Once you have crystallized a mission for each platform of interest, it's time to adjust your focus. The entire social network will not be interested in your content, which is why it is immensely important to hone in on your followers, fans and advocates. Figure out where your ideal audience resides and spark a conversation. Natural engagement is an instant endorsement of your talent brand. Reinforce your connection among employees, consumers and potential candidates by fostering a consistent, approachable brand voice. Your content style should be developed in such a way that you can be easily distinguished from your competitors.

## 3. Socialize!

Social media is a two-way street. It's not enough to just create and publish compelling content; you must interact with those who engage with you. Grow your social authority by sharing relevant content, taking inspiration from other industries, being open to conversation and connecting with those who have a voice and influence within your industry. It's not always easy to capture someone's attention, but a simple act such as sharing a post or 'favouriting' a tweet can enhance the human element, increase your approachability and allow you to stand apart from the competition. Most importantly, be consistent with your posting and keep your finger on the pulse!

Build a social calendar with content and imagery that tells your brand story. For example, consider featuring:

- Visuals of the work environment, both inside and outside.
- A message from your CEO.
- Business milestones and goals achieved.
- Employee testimonials.
- Visuals of your team working, collaborating and perhaps even socializing.

### 4. Set your goals and track your metrics

Social media marketing is more than just hashtags and retweets. Besides creating best-in-class content, it is equally important to track the influence of your messaging with reliable metrics. Once you've set those achievable and impactful social media goals that we just discussed, and developed your campaigns, the next step is to analyse the referrals, conversions, likes, comments, shares and mentions against your advertising and talent branding efforts.

Content is the key to any great talent brand. Although it is ever-changing and takes steady effort, a refined social media strategy can foster new business relationships, boost employee morale, highlight your capabilities and increase brand exposure, awareness and word-of-mouth.

# Social Media Marketing Brief

What are you looking to achieve via social media?

Who is your target audience?

What do you want the audience to think or do after visiting a social media site?

What are the two or three most important topics or areas of focus you'd like to share across various social media platforms?

What are some key dates and events planned this year that you want to bring attention to and create buzz around?

Which social media site do you feel is essential to your current business model? Conversely, are there social media sites that you don't want to be associated with?

Which social media tactics have you seen and liked? Which have you disliked?

Are you interested in expanding into blogs? Do you want to publish (and are you capable of maintaining) timely newsletters and white papers?

How will you measure the success of your social media campaign – traffic, signups, likes/fans/followers/retweets, comments, applications?

Who do you see as competition for your business/talent needs?

List any forums, blogs or people that are popular within your industry for providing real-time news and information.

Do you have any 'must-haves' or 'must-not-haves' for your social media presence?

**Process and interaction**
What is your current hiring process? What can the candidate expect to happen once they apply, and beyond?

What are some of your most effective, least costly recruitment strategies?

From your perspective, what makes the company a wonderful place to work?

Are you affiliated with any charitable organizations?

What is your social archetype?

How often would you like to create and post content?

What relevant groups, blogs or other forums are you an active member of?

What are the most important characteristics you look for when hiring someone?

What is the approval process for use of imagery that does not come from your marketing team?

What is the response procedure for content that gets posted to the site?

Will you have anyone on staff in charge of communicating with your social community through forums, comments and feeds on a daily basis?

What is your overall budget for implementation, and your monthly maintenance budget?

What is the production schedule for your social media presence, including a launch date and readiness for key events?

Will you be able to supply all of the content required?

# TO OPEN OR NOT TO OPEN – EMAIL MARKETING BEST PRACTICES

Email marketing remains king; despite the digital competition, this tried-and-true channel is still as relevant as ever. You are six times more likely to get a click-through from an email campaign than you are from a tweet. As one of the oldest, yet still top-performing digital marketing practices, email marketing can be a driving force behind amplifying your recruitment efforts and talent brand. The goal of a thriving campaign is to build the talent pipeline, drive candidate interest and engagement, and continuously support your employer value proposition.

## Segment your communications

Needless to say, the vast majority of the content you provide will not be of interest to each and every individual on your subscription list. Targeted communication transforms potential candidates into viable applicants. Each candidate is going through a different journey within the hiring process, whether it is discovery, interest or pursuance. Your objective should be to keep their interest at every stage, sending the right content and messaging at the right time. Providing valuable and significant content and opportunities to candidates based on their interests and experiences enhances the candidate experience.

## Disrupt your audience

How do you communicate with those who opt in? How are you continuing to build and nurture that relationship? These are questions that should spearhead your efforts. Your audience always has two options: to open or not to open, to click or not to click, and so on. Which element of your content is going to influence them to follow through on your call to action? Your campaigns should ensure that your emails are successfully delivered, opened, read and clicked through. The first step in capturing the attention of an audience within an overflowing inbox is a compelling and informative subject line. The key is to create a sense of urgency, referencing key words, locations and names. Once you've made the personal connection and enticed them to open, include relevant details, highlight key words and use bold subheadings. Add multiple calls to actions and click-through links within the beginning, middle and end of the email. That way, your audience has the option and authority to choose when they want more information from you.

## Always be testing

Analysing the data derived from your content is just as important as creating it. This will allow you to optimize your strategy and customize the context of your emails. Segment your contacts in order of topic and interest, test your delivery times to create a consistent delivery schedule, and A/B test your subject line to engage without having to create a completely new message. Improving metrics like opens, click, leads, impressions, conversions, bounces and reads will allow you to know exactly what to send to whom, at what time, and how often.

## Always be branding

Brands that personalize marketing emails experience higher click rates and higher open rates than those that do not. Whether you are sending a newsletter, hot new job alert or thank-you email, all of your content should be consistently branded. Your design template should be customized with your logo, brand colours, a footer with hyperlinks leading back to your site, and custom social media links to ensure that your content is shareable. Leave your stamp on your content and in the minds of your candidates!

# EVALUATING YOUR EFFORTS THROUGH METRICS

Elsewhere in the book I mentioned the key criteria used when we evaluate our talent branding efforts.

Our Benchmark:

- Is it authentic, or is it appealing to a wide variety of audiences, and does it truly represent your global culture? Will the expectations, benefits and employee experience you are portraying be confirmed across social channels, referrals and word-of-mouth?
- Is it aligned with your corporate brand, mission, values and business objectives? Is it globally consistent, yet flexible enough to accommodate different regional and talent segments?
- Is it differentiated, or does it represent the special qualities that make your organization unique, and more appealing to the people you want to attract than any of their other prospects?
- Is it emotive? Does it inspire people to come to work, perform at their best and recommend your organization to other talented professionals?
- Does it have staying power? It may be true today, but will it still be valid 3-5 years from now?

A wide variety of metrics are used by organizations to measure the return on their branding efforts.

These include tracking things like:

- Open-to-fill.
- Cost per candidate.
- Increased number of hires.
- Cost per hire.
- Time to fill.
- Increased number of applicants/interviews/candidates.
- Increased number of employee referrals.
- Quality of hire.
- Employee engagement.
- Careers site traffic.
- Careers site time on site.
- Social engagement (likes, shares, retweets).
- Increased retention/decreased turnover.

Some measurements might be more business-oriented than HR-oriented, such as social sentiment, CEO approval increase, increased revenue or customer loyalty.

Or, one of my favourites: how many people are you hiring away from your competitors?

Choose the ones you feel might be right for you, and then establish and hold to a reporting schedule that makes the most sense based on which metrics you've selected. The talent branding process never ends – you just keep refining, enhancing and building equity in your organization as a best place to work.

# BUSTING
# THE MYTHS

Considering how important talent branding is, I still encounter a lot of confusion and misinformation about it. So, as a public service, I thought I'd bust some of the myths.

## Myth #1: Talent branding is unnecessary

Some clients tell me, "We're an employer of choice; great candidates will find us." And yet you never hear executives at Apple or Disney or Coke say, "Everyone knows and loves our products; customers will find us." In fact, those brands have massive marketing budgets. You can't assume that your precise desired demographic, whether it's MIT graduates or truck drivers, will actively seek you out. Or think about this: What if great candidates *do* know you, but *don't like what they see?* Talent branding can increase awareness and engagement by refocusing your image as an employer.

## Myth #2: Talent branding is expensive

Talent branding actually *saves* you money, through lower recruiting costs, higher engagement and increased productivity/sales. Depending on the plan goals, a basic research project can be launched for as little as $10,000. You can start small with communication audits and internal surveys, and then add executive interviews and employee focus groups. If you can secure a larger spend, we recommend surveying external constituents to provide context for your internal findings.

## Myth #3: Talent branding is completely separate from consumer branding

It better not be! One of the first things we do on any talent branding project is break through organizational silos and align the employer's talent brand with the company's current messaging.

We try to get all stakeholders – Marketing, HR, Internal Communications – into the same room to make sure we have a consistent brand that's authentic on both sides of the house. Along the way, we often help Marketing and HR become friends! A talent brand must be absolutely aligned with and inspired by the consumer brand. After all, candidates are customers, investors and influencers of every stripe.

## Myth #4: Talent branding research can be done in-house

It *can*, but it's much more difficult. Employees are reluctant to share their true feelings with their HR department for fear of reprisal. Having executives interview each other often leads to an 'echo chamber' effect, where no one advocates change. And external constituents, such as customers and former applicants, think surveys are a marketing ploy and stay away. An outside set of eyes can reveal things about your talent brand that you never saw.

## Myth #5: Talent branding only helps the hiring managers

Au contraire! The entire company benefits from a strong talent brand. You'll attract employees who are a good fit for the culture, stay longer, perform better and recommend the company to others. More referrals and lower turnover makes for a happier, more stable workplace. HR will have more time to work on other initiatives, such as workforce planning, talent management or diversity. Eventually, you'll have weeded out the underachievers and filled your roster with high performing employees, which studies have shown generate more profit for the entire organization.

Don't let these myths fool you. Talent branding is crucial to the success of any company, from a non-profit to a regional chain to a global corporation. It cuts costs, generates profits and can turn your company into a true employer of choice.

# IN
# CONCLUSION

## Recruiting, talent branding and everyone you know

A positive talent brand can help attract top candidates, making recruiting for your top positions easier. But, candidates don't come to us in a vacuum. Before they even apply for a position or speak to a recruiter, they've been exposed to advertising, the experience of family members or friends, and the power of social media to shape what they know, or think they know, about your business. In fact, according to a recent survey, word-of-mouth is the most powerful factor in consumers' relationships with brands.[17]

Companies are looking to have more control over the impression they make in the minds of applicants. And those who have succeeded have been guided by the same methods and techniques used by consumer branding agencies. Moving beyond simple brainstorming sessions between Talent Acquisition teams and/ or Internal Communications, the research methods used to glean employee information and create talent brands have now expanded to commonly include employee surveys, focus groups and in-depth executive interviews. Even so, in today's highly social world, with low unemployment and the competition for talent a top concern for CEOs everywhere, that still might not be enough.

Today's talent branding considers employer branding a two-way street, as the employee and candidate experience is shareable (almost viral) and transparency and authenticity are the table stakes.

---

17  "Ogilvy Cannes Study: Behold the Power of Word of Mouth," Accessed June, 2017, http://www.adweek.com/digital/ogilvy-cannes-study-behold-the-power-of-word-of-mouth/?red=pr/

Talent branding can be seen as the evolution of employer branding. At its best, it is the art of making a strong emotional connection from your organization and its culture to the talent it needs to attract to drive the business forward. And while the visible output of the efforts may be the same – a redesigned or enhanced website, recruiting booths, brochures or website banners – the research and development process has been refined to be as inclusive as possible of all audiences and all available information.

We are seeing a greater emphasis on both the employee *experience*, the candidate *experience* and the development of personalized messages that can speak to the wants and needs of each of our audiences at every phase of the hiring process. That extends all the way through to candidate rejection and employee termination.

What salaries are you paying? What interview questions are you asking? How do people rate the talents and abilities of your CEO? The answers to these questions are so easily obtained that we take them for granted, yet we may not give enough thought to the implications and responsibility this all places on recruiters, hiring managers and even our employees themselves.

If you are about to embark on a talent branding initiative, here's how you can build a bullet-proof talent brand and take things to the next level.

## 1. Expand your research

a. When doing talent brand research, consider external and competitive research as well. Don't just speak to the people inside your company; also take a look at the external landscape.

b. Which companies are the competitors for your top talent? What are the appealing aspects of their employment offer? This can be easy enough to find out by going to their website and social sites and even pursuing LinkedIn and Glassdoor. What awards have they won and which groups are they targeting with unique messages (military veterans, women, other diverse groups)?

## 2. Consider every touch point

a. Take a view of every touch point in the candidate's consideration process and see what you have (or need) to influence their decision in your favour.

b. Consider how you are moving talent through the hiring process along with managing the feelings of those you're no longer interested in.

c. Beyond supplying top prospects with materials or links to your website, create an information funnel designed for people with small, medium and large appetites for details about the company, the culture, the business strategy and what their day-to-day work would really look like. Make sure that when you develop the content you've replicated it across all media – video, digital, PowerPoint, email and print. And, ensure that you've rolled each of these out across all social channels.

## 3. Influence the influencers

a. As we evolve from employer branding to talent branding, this is probably the most important take-away. Simply put, everyone is an influencer. Your current employees, alumni and thought leaders. Parents, spouses and friends. Vendors, customers and just about everyone you know.

b. Make sure you've thought carefully about your talent brand (the things that make your company, culture and offerings unique), the wants and desires of the people you're trying to reach, and very importantly, how your stories are told, retold, refuted and shared in a world gone social.

Only then will you have truly mastered the art of The Talent Brand.

# APPENDIX
# DOCUMENTS

# The Talent Brand Development Process

While every project is different, we follow the same four-step methodology for all the talent brand development work we perform: Define, Align, Design and Refine.

## Define

Meet with project stakeholders:

- Define goals and campaign objectives.
- Review current strategy documents/relevant materials.
- Discuss usage and audience of current/new materials.

Launch communications audit:

- Website.
- Printed materials, newsletters and brochures.
- Recent press releases.
- Trade show banners and booth materials.
- Current advertising, both conventional and online, including social media.
- Advertising venues and channels.
- Media calendar and buys.
- URLs, keywords.

Launch primary research:

- Focus groups, executive interviews, secret shoppers, in-depth interviews, customer intercepts etc.

### Align

Ensure that all brand alignment opportunities are optimized:
- Visual brand palette.
- Brand vocabulary.
- Available photos/videos and other assets.

### Design

Create talent brand architecture and framework:
- Develop a brand identity to be used as the cornerstone of all advertising and marketing communications.
- Analyse and prioritize the communications needs and implement a precise timeline and budget for each.

### Refine

Conduct weekly or monthly on-site or phone conferences with key project stakeholders to review and support upcoming initiatives.

# Research Guides

## Employee Focus Groups

Sample invitation:

**Subject: We want to hear your thoughts...**

Dear Employee,

In an effort to brand the (Company) experience to attract and retain the best talent as we grow, we are seeking the assistance of the people who know it best: the employees of (Company).

You have been selected to participate in a 90–120 minute discussion with several of your colleagues. We have engaged a third-party agency to hold an anonymous, open forum where you can share the benefits of our culture and the value of working here.

Here are the details: (Date)/(Time)/(Location).

Thank you in advance for your participation. As a token of our gratitude you will receive (incentive goes here) at the end of the session.

If you have any questions, or are unable to attend, please contact (Name) at (phone #).

We are excited to hear from you!

# Employee Focus Group Discussion Guide

### Set-up
- One large table.
- Name cards.
- Pads/pens.
- Flip-charts/markers.

### Objective
- Understand employee perceptions and attitudes toward the company as an employer.
- Explore:
  - ▷ Identity, culture and personality.
  - ▷ Reasons for joining and staying.

### Guidelines
- Make yourself comfortable, this will be fun.
- Bring the energy.
- No cell phones!
- Feel free to step out if you need to use the rest room.

### Warm up and explanation
The purpose of this group is to learn about your experience working in this company and gain insight into the value proposition that makes it a desirable workplace for talented employees.

Please remember, we are interested in your real, unfiltered opinions, so do not feel you must edit them in any way. Nobody outside this room will be able to attribute any of your remarks back to you.

My name is (Name) and I will be the group moderator for this session. As moderator, I will assist in the discussions and keep the group on track. I may have to interrupt conversations at times in the interest of covering everything in our limited time together. This will not reflect on your content or my personal viewpoint.

Thanks for helping!

## Introductions
Let's start by going around the table. Please introduce yourself, and include:
- Your first name, position and length of service.

## Discussion
- How did you find out about the job opportunity?
- Did you know anything about the company before you joined?
- If yes, who told you? If not, where did you go to learn more about it?
- What surprised you the most about the company?

## Company
- In one sentence, what does this company do?
- What are the most important things to know about succeeding within this environment?
- What would you characterize as management's expectations?
- What do you receive in return?

## Exercise 1: Culture

**On the sticky notes in front of you, write three adjectives that:**
- Best describe the company's culture.
- Best describe how you feel at work.
- Best describe the people who succeed here.

(Probe responses such as: integrity, delivers on commitments, continuously strives to improve, freely contributes ideas and adds value, is positive and encouraging, exhibits flexibility and urgency.)

Have each respondent read their answers out loud and open for discussion.

- What celebrity, real or fictional, would best represent the ideal employee company? Why?
- Who wouldn't do well in this environment?

Imagine you are on an aeroplane talking to the passenger seated next to you, who happens to be an IT professional looking for a new job. They could get a job anywhere, but you stand to receive a $5,000 bonus for successfully referring him/her to the company.

- What would you tell this person to get them to join the company?
- Is there something you wouldn't tell them because it might change their mind?

## Discussion

- What are the things that excite and energize you about your work?
- Imagine your best friend began working here. What would you tell him or her are the unwritten rules they won't find in the employee handbook?
- Where do you see the company in five years?
  - ▷ Do you expect to still be with the company?

## Employer attributes

### When considering other opportunities, what is most important to you? (unaided)

(Probe)
Advancement opportunities.
Pay and benefits.
Job security.
Work/Life balance.
Leadership.
Great co-workers.
Learning and development.

### How does (Company) measure up?

If you received a good offer from another company, what if anything would keep you here?

If you left, what would you miss the most?

The company's vision is to (insert company vision).

### On a scale of 1 to 5 – with 5 being the best – how well do you think you fulfil the vision today?

## Exercise 2: Positioning exercise (handout)

## The 'World's Best Job Fair' recruiting booth

Imagine you're exhibiting at a job fair that is populated by the very best and brightest potential employees. With intense competition for the attendees' hearts and minds, what three words or word-groups would you display in your booth to help attract top talent to the company?

## Exercise 3: Ten minutes with the company president

For our final exercise, imagine you had ten minutes with the company president where you could anonymously say anything you'd want him to know. What would you say?

# Executive Interviews

## Sample Invitation

## Subject: We want to hear your thoughts...

Dear (Colleague),

In an effort to brand the (Company) experience to attract and retain the best talent as we grow, we are seeking the assistance of those who know it best: the employees of (Company). We will be hosting several focus groups for them to share their thoughts and experiences.

As an executive of (Company) and valued contributor to our financial success, we are asking for your insights as well. You are invited to participate in a 30-minute phone or in-person conversation. The topics will include your thoughts on our business, our culture and our talent.

Below are dates and times when these one-on-one interviews will be conducted. Please contact (Name) at (phone number) and confirm your availability, and whether you prefer a phone call or in-person meeting.

Thank you in advance for your participation, and please do not hesitate to contact me should you have any questions.

# Executive Interview Discussion Guide

## Warm up and explanation

As you may know, we are currently working on an initiative to develop a talent brand. Our work will expand on our talent acquisition and retention efforts by defining what makes (Company) different, marketable and a great place to work.

As one of the driving forces behind (Company's) business success, I would like to hear your thoughts on our organization and its culture and talent.

## Respondent information:

- What is your role?
- When did you join the organization?
- Have you ever worked for another company in this industry? If so, how is (Company) different?
- Do you consider the company to be successful?
- If so, what do you see as the three key reasons for its success?
- Which three words would you want people to associate with your organization?

## Brand

- What does the company promise to its customers?
- Does it always deliver? If not, why?

## Employee

- What three adjectives best describe your corporate culture?
- Does it vary by location, entity or position?
- What do the company's best employees have in common?
- What kinds of people won't do well here?
- What does (Company) promise its employees?
- What do you expect from them in return?
- What are the things that make building a career with (Company) a unique experience?

## Marketplace

- How do you see the organization changing in the next 2-3 years?
- What might you need to change within the company's culture or work to support those changes?
- If you could wave a magic wand and make one change within the organization, what would that be?
- What inspires you?
- What has been your proudest moment professionally?

# Talent Brand Employee Survey

## Invitation

### Subject: We want to hear your thoughts...

Dear (Name),

Having the best and brightest talent on our team is critical to maintaining our leadership position in our industry. That's why we are making it a priority to understand our talent brand: what makes us different and marketable from an employment perspective and what the key drivers of our culture are.

We'd like to invite you to share your perspective. To do so, we've created an anonymous online survey to help us determine what our employees value most. It's attached below.

Completing this short, anonymous survey will take no more than ten minutes, but the results will be invaluable in helping us best portray ourselves as an employer of choice within the talent community.

Click here to begin the survey (link).

The results will be analysed by an outside company and, as promised, your response will be completely confidential.

Thanks for your time.

Sincerely,
(Name)

## Survey

**Please tell us a bit about yourself:**

1. **Your gender**
   - Male.
   - Female.

2. **Your age**
   - <20.
   - 21-30.
   - 31-40.
   - 41-50.
   - >50.

3. **Your role:**

4. **How long have you worked for (Company)?**
   - Less than a year.
   - 1-3 years.
   - 4-6 years.
   - 7-10 years.
   - >10 years.

5. **If you were recommending career opportunities to a friend, which three things would they most likely be swayed by:**
   Compensation and benefits.
   Career advancement potential.
   Training and development.
   Work/life balance.
   A fun and friendly work environment.
   An opportunity to work remotely.
   The company's ethics and integrity.

The quality of co-workers.
The company mission and impact.
The quality of the organization's leaders.
Corporate reputation.
None of the above.

Other:

6. **Rank each of the entries within each category in order of importance to you, by marking a '1' next to the most important, '2' next to the second-most important, etc.**

- **Status**
  Prestigious name recognition.
  Market leadership.
  Secure employment.
  Quality of products and services.

- **Work**
  Challenging work.
  Customer focus.
  Performance recognized by management and peers.

- **Career opportunities**
  Clear path for advancement.
  Leadership opportunities.
  Rapid promotion.

- **Learning**
  Professional training and development.
  Leaders who provide coaching and feedback.
  Variety of assignments.

- **Purpose**
  Corporate responsibility.
  Inspiring management.
  Ethical standards.

- **People**
  Working with the best talent.
  Team-oriented work.
  Respect for people.
  Friendly working environment.

- **Empowerment**
  High level of responsibility.
  Personal interests enabled.
  Flexible work/life balance.

- **Innovation**
  Creative/dynamic environment.
  Fast growing, entrepreneurial.
  Innovative.

- **Rewards**
  Competitive compensation.
  Great benefits.
  Generous vacation allowance.

7. **Which of the following words or phrases best evoke the company culture? (Circle up to five.)**

| | |
|---|---|
| Corporate | Caring |
| Ethical | Relevant |
| Community-oriented | Stimulating |
| Collaborative | Old-school |
| Empowering | Engaging |
| Frustrating | Fast-paced |
| Fun | Structured |
| Conservative | Innovative |
| Demanding | Adaptive |
| Consistent | Inspiring |
| Customer-focused | Stable |
| Secretive | Confusing |
| Fearful | Respectful |
| Responsible | Struggling |
| Professional | Family-friendly |
| Cohesive | Profit-driven |

8. **Which of the following words or phrases best evoke how you feel working at the company? (Circle up to four.)**

| | |
|---|---|
| Accomplished. | Passionate. |
| Anxious. | Valued. |
| Confident. | Confused. |
| Empowered. | Uncertain. |
| Frustrated. | Listened to. |
| Happy. | Rewarded. |
| Overwhelmed. | Supported. |
| Overworked. | Underutilized. |
| Safe. | |

9. **Pick the character that best describes the company. (Circle one.)**
   - The Regular Guy/Gal: humble, hard-working and friendly.
   - The Ruler: leading people through confidence, determination and influence.
   - The Sage: using intelligence and analysis to understand the world.
   - The Hero: using expert mastery in a way that improves the world.
   - The Revolutionary: committed to overturning what isn't working.
   - The Magician: making things happen.
   - The Partner: being in a relationship with the people, work and surroundings they love.
   - The Caregiver: protecting and caring for others.
   - The Creator: creating things of enduring value.

10. **Overall, how happy are you working for the company? (Circle one.)**
   Completely happy.
   Very happy.
   Somewhat happy.
   Neutral.
   Somewhat unhappy.
   Very unhappy.
   Completely unhappy.

11. **How has your overall job happiness changed from when you started? (Circle one.)**
   Happiness increased / happiness decreased / no change.

12. **Would you recommend this company as a great place to work? (Circle one.)**
   Yes / No.

# Testing Output with Internal/External Audiences

### Introduction to research
- Welcome and introduction to the purpose of research.
- Explanation of how their feedback will be used to refine the company's creative messaging.
- Housekeeping: no cell phones, no side conversations, be honest, have fun.

### Creative concepts
- Describe in your own words what you think of this concept.
- How does it make you feel about the company?
- What if anything stands out?
- Do you have any specific likes?
- Do you have any specific dislikes?
- What do you think of the copy?
- What do you think of the imagery?
- What do you think of the layout?
- What's the main message you take away from this creative work?
- Do you feel it represents the company? Does it ring true?
- Who do you think this concept would appeal to?
- In what ways could it be improved?
- Is there anything missing?
- Do you think the message offers something different from the company's competitors?
- Do you think this creative concept would motivate you to find out more about careers at the company? Why/why not?

*Repeat for each concept.*

## Indicating preference

- Taking everything into account, which is your preferred concept? And why?
- Before we finish, rate the elements of the creative concepts. Assign a rating of 1-5, with 5 being excellent, for each of these:
  ▷ The copy.
  ▷ The image.
  ▷ The message.
  ▷ The layout.
  ▷ The overall concept.

Thank you for your participation.

# Focus Group Icebreakers and Exercises

We all love icebreakers because they warm up the conversation and refocus the purpose of the event at hand. Whether the aim is to provide an introduction, team building, brainstorming or the exploration of a particular topic, icebreakers set the tone when working toward a common goal. The key to a successful session is a well thought-out exercise that increases engagement, encourages contribution and keeps the objective top-of-mind. Below are a few great ones to kick off your focus groups and put your participants in the right frame of mind.

## Career success moments

Begin by asking each participant to think about a highlight of their career that they would want to re-experience, how they felt, and why. This first part lets participants reflect back on their careers, while the second helps them get to know their co-workers on a more intimate level.

## ABC, this is me

Ask each employee to write their name vertically on a sheet of paper, and then list one word horizontally that starts with each letter of their name, to describe specific company characteristics. This is a fun way to easily create a master list of what people see as the outstanding traits of the company.

## If I could have, I would have

Books and movies abound with stories of people seeking different paths in their lives, and almost everyone has wished at some point that they'd done something different. Ask each person to describe an alternative path they might have taken. Probe on how life on the path-not-taken might have been different from the one they pursued.

### First or worst
Have each participant share their first – or worst – job. Probe on how that work experience differed from their current one or helped shape what they're seeking in a job. This sparks conversation, and participants can have some fun telling tales of their past endeavours.

### If I were a brand
Going around the room, ask participants to share which brand they would want to be and why. Probe on the emotive qualities that shape their response (powerful, reliable, confident) rather than any functional/rational reasons (low-cost, convenient, well-known).

### What if
Ask participants to think about where they would be working if their current employer was no longer in business. Probe on why, and what they would miss the most. This exercise might reveal great insights into how the competition is perceived and what might be unique about their current company's culture.

### The unwritten rules of the employee handbook
Ask participants to share something they wish they'd known about their employer, or specific job, before they started. Follow through on what they were most surprised about, what they'd tell their best friend about the job in advance of the friend's start date, or what might be missing from the employee handbook that everyone knows but no one talks about.

### At the barbecue
Ask participants to describe their current employer as if they were doing so with their friends or strangers in a casual party-like setting. Probe on whether what they'd say would be different for various audiences. For extra fun, see who can describe it in the fewest words.

## The 'World's Best Job Fair' recruiting booth

As suggested earlier, imagine you're exhibiting at a job fair that's attended by the best possible candidates. In this intensely competitive setting, what three words, or word-groups, would you use to attract top talent to your organization?

# RESOURCES

While in no way intended to be a complete list, check out the following links for helpful contacts, ideas, tools and other resources.

## TALENT AND EMPLOYER BRAND LINKEDIN GROUPS

| | |
|---|---|
| Employer Branding | https://www.linkedin.com/groups/37264 |
| EBI: Employer Branding Global Community | https://www.linkedin.com/groups/1338647 |
| Employer Branding w/ HR | https://www.linkedin.com/groups/8427902 |
| Recruitment Consultants and Staffing Professionals | https://www.linkedin.com/groups/52762 |
| Employee Advocacy | https://www.linkedin.com/groups/5063283 |
| Human Resources Network (HRN) | https://www.linkedin.com/groups/7042470 |
| Employee Experience Management | https://www.linkedin.com/groups/8585034 |
| Innovations in HR | https://www.linkedin.com/groups/8574511 |

| | |
|---|---|
| Hands-On Employer Branding | https://www.linkedin.com/groups/2738973 |
| ERE.net | https://www.linkedin.com/groups/33809 |
| Brand and Communications Management | https://www.linkedin.com/groups/64854 |
| Employee Communications and Engagement | https://www.linkedin.com/groups/59169 |
| Branding Professionals | https://www.linkedin.com/groups/116821 |
| Talent Acquisition Executive | https://www.linkedin.com/groups/131881 |
| Global Employer Brand Management | https://www.linkedin.com/groups/1161417 |
| Internal Branding 2.0 | https://www.linkedin.com/groups/2694464 |
| Internal Communications Challenges | https://www.linkedin.com/groups/2358636 |

## CONFERENCES

| | |
|---|---|
| Social Recruiting Strategies | http://socialrecruitingstrategies.com/ |
| Glassdoor Summit | http://resources.glassdoor.com/summit-2016-livestream-recordings-register.html |
| Employer Branding Strategies | http://www.employerbrandingstrategies.com/chicago-2017/ |
| Indeed Interactive | http://indeedinteractive.com/ |
| HRTech | http://www.hrtechconference.com/ |
| HRO Today | http://www.hrotodayforum.com/ |
| Talent42 | http://talent42.com/ |
| The Employer Branding Conference | http://www.employerbrandingconference.com/region-sa |
| RecruitCon | http://recruitcon.blr.com/ |

| | |
|---|---|
| Strategic Talent Acquisition | http://www.hci.org/hr-conferences/2017-Strategic-Talent-Acquisition/overview |
| ERE | https://www.eremedia.com/events/ |
| LinkedIn Talent Connect | https://business.linkedin.com/events/talent-connect#! |
| Inbound | http://www.inbound.com/ |
| SHRM | https://annual.shrm.org/ |
| Transform | http://transformrecruitmentmarketing.com/ |
| Employer Branding Day | https://www.worldemployerbrandingday.community/ |
| Recruiting Trends | http://www.recruitingtrendsconf.com/ |
| AchievEE | http://www.achievee.org/ |

## TWITTER HASHTAGS

#EBCHAT
#EBJobs
#Tchat
#employerbranding
#recruitmentmarketing
#socialrecruiting
#talentacquisition
#socialrecruitment
#NextWaveEB
#employeeengagement

## TOOLS

Thanks to technology, there are a considerable number of talent branding and communications tools on the market today. Below are some of the more established players.

| | | |
|---|---|---|
| BufferApp | Social Media Strategy | https://buffer.com/ |
| Canva | Graphic Design Tools | https://www.canva.com/ |
| Dynamic Signal | Company Comms Platform | http://dynamicsignal.com/ |
| Fluid Surveys | Online Survey Platform | http://fluidsurveys.com/ |
| Gaggle Amp | Employee Advocacy System | https://www.gaggleamp.com/# |
| Greenhouse | Modern Recruiting Software | https://www.greenhouse.io/ |
| Hootsuite | Social Media Strategy | https://hootsuite.com/ |

| | | |
|---|---|---|
| ICIMS | Social Media Recruiting Tools: 6 Networking Sites You Need to Use | https://www.icims.com/hiring-insights/for-employers/article-social-media-recruiting-tools-6-networking-sites-you-need-to#sm.0000qjtkjf9occtzyy72lp818juot |
| Lever | Modern Recruiting Software | https://www.lever.co/ |
| Mix Panel | Analytics Platform | https://mixpanel.com/ |
| MOZ | SEO Tracking and Research Toolset | https://moz.com/ |
| Next Wave Hire | Recruiting Platform | http://www.nextwavehire.com/ |
| Phenom People | Talent Relationship Marketing (TRM) | http://www.phenompeople.com/ |
| Rebel Mouse | Content Management System | https://www.rebelmouse.com/ |
| Small Improvements | Employee Feedback Software | https://www.small-improvements.com/ |
| Smashfly | Recruitment Marketing Platform | http://www.smashfly.com/resources/ |

| So Go Survey | Online Survey Platform | https://www.sogosurvey.com/ |
| Sprout Social | Social Media Strategy | http://sproutsocial.com/ |
| Survey Gizmo | Online Survey Platform | https://www.surveygizmo.com/ |
| Survey Hero | Online Survey Platform | https://www.surveyherocom/?gclid=CMrpxKrF6tICFUiHswodoaEPVA |
| Survey Monkey | Online Survey Platform | https://www.surveymonkey.com/ |
| Survey Planet | Online Survey Platform | https://surveyplanet.com/ |
| TINYpulse | Employee Reention, Engagement, and Performance Software | https://www.tinypulse.com/ |
| Tweetdeck | Social Media Strategy | https://tweetdeck.twitter.com |
| Zoho | Online Survey Platform | https://www.zoho.com/survey/ |

# AN INTRODUCTION TO
# JODY ORDIONI

**Jody Ordioni** is the founder and chief brand officer of Brandemix. a branding agency that solves business challenges through defining and marketing organizational culture to the people who drive business forward.